Dreaming of Rose

Also published by Handheld Press

Dreaming of Rose

A Biographer's Journal

By Sarah LeFanu

Handheld Research 5

First published in 2013.
This edition published in 2021 by Handheld Press
72 Warminster Road, Bath BA2 6RU, United Kingdom.
www.handheldpress.co.uk

ISBN 978-1-912766-52-9

1 2 3 4 5 6 7 8 9 0

Series design by Nadja Guggi and typeset in Open Sans.

Printed and bound in Great Britain by TJ Books Limited, Padstow.

For Mon,
friend and travelling companion

Sarah LeFanu, who is distantly related to the Victorian Gothic novelist Sheridan Le Fanu, was born in Aberdeen and was brought up in Scotland and East Africa. She is the author of *Something of Themselves: Kipling, Kingsley, Conan Doyle and the Anglo-Boer War* (2020), *S Is for Samora: A Lexical Biography of Samora Machel and the Mozambican Dream* (2012), *Rose Macaulay: A Biography* (2003), and *In the Chinks of the World Machine: Feminism and Science Fiction* (1988), which won the MLA Emily Toth Award.

She has taught creative writing for many years, was Artistic Director of the Bath Literature Festival for 2004–2009, was a senior editor at The Women's Press and has presented programmes for BBC Radio 4. She lives near Bristol in North Somerset.

Contents

Acknowledgements

A shorter version of Chapter Nine was published in the *Arvon Journal*, Winter 2001; 'The Biographer's Journey', based on the same chapter, was broadcast on BBC Radio 3, 8 June 2003, read by the author and produced by Sara Davies. The Epilogue, 'About the *Letters*', is a revised version of the Epilogue to *Rose Macaulay: A Biography* (2003).

Some names have been changed.

List of illustrations

All efforts have been made to trace copyright holders of uncredited images. Please contact the publishers if additional permission needs to be arranged.

1. Cover of writing journal with fishes. Newnham College, Cambridge.

2. Rose Macaulay as a Caterpillar in 'Privilege of Parliament' from the Somerville College 1903 Going-Down Play. By kind permission of the Principal and Fellows of Somerville College, Oxford.

3. Varazze and a crowded sea, around 1900, from a contemporary postcard. Comune di Varraze.

4. Contemporary photograph of the procession on the Feast of Santa Caterina, Varazze. Comune di Varraze.

5. Sketch of Marjorie Grant Cook. By kind permission of Dr Mary Anne O'Donovan.

6. Constance Babington Smith at work during the Second World War, studying an air reconnaissance photograph for evidence of the V1 rocket. *Times*, 11 August 2000.

7. Sarah LeFanu receiving an Arts Council Award from Salman Rushdie, June 2001. Richard H Smith.

8. Ivy Compton-Burnett. Claude Harris.

9. A plate from the Yeşilyurt Otel, Trebizond, and crest detail. Sarah LeFanu.

10. The Byzantine arches in the ruins at Trebizond. Sarah LeFanu.

11. The photograph of Rose Macaulay in her flat in the 1950s, now on display at the London Library.

12. The *Daily Mail* article, 'Did this priest betray this woman?', 12 October 1961.

13. The portrait of Father Jeremiah in the Temperance Hall, Loughrea, Galway. Sarah LeFanu.

14. Rose Macaulay photographed in Venice in 1957, with no priests visible. Roloff Beny.

15. Constance Babington Smith, at the time the *Letters* were published. Gerry Bauer.

Family Tree of Rose Macaulay

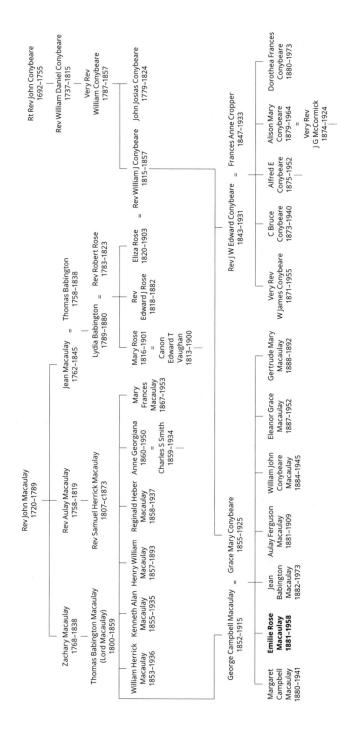

Preface

Rose Macaulay was one of the few English women of the first half of the twentieth century to earn her living entirely through her writing. Throughout the 1920s, 1930s and 1940s she was close to the heart of literary and political life in Britain, observing, participating in, and satirising it. She was friends with Ivy Compton-Burnett, Elizabeth Bowen (who was first published through her recommendation), Rosamond Lehmann, and, at times, Virginia Woolf. She was also friends with E M Forster (and wrote the first full-length critical book on his work), with Walter de la Mare, T S Eliot and Victor Gollancz. She sat on committees for the National Council for Civil Liberties and the Peace Pledge Union, with Forster and Storm Jameson and Stephen Spender, and in 1928 she was one of the thirty-nine witnesses for the defence at the trial for obscenity of Radclyffe Hall's novel *The Well of Loneliness*. She wrote for the *Spectator*, *Time and Tide*, the *New Statesman* and for John Lehmann's *New Writing*. She broadcast regularly for the BBC from its inception in the early 1920s through to the 1950s. Under the chairmanship of George Bernard Shaw, she was on the BBC Standing Committee on Spoken English during the 1930s and 1940s.

Wherever you look in English literary life, in any decade in the first half of the twentieth century, there you see the lean figure of Rose Macaulay. But you see her in no one place centrally, nor for long. 'Forever in transit', said Rosamond Lehmann of her, 'physically, intellectually, spiritually' (quoted in Babington Smith 1972, 225).

In a writing career that lasted fifty years, Rose Macaulay produced twenty-three novels (three of which won major literary prizes), six books of essays and criticism, four books of travel and history, and two collections of poetry. She left behind a large correspondence, from which four volumes of letters have been published. Her fiction alone shows an enormous range: from family drama to social satire, from fantasy to stream-of-consciousness. The novels that came out of the years of the First World War, *Non-Combatants and Others* (1916), *What Not* (1918) and *Potterism* (1920), all engaged in different ways with the reality of war well in advance of the novels and memoirs by male writers that have since become the canonical works of the period.

Non-Combatants and Others was one of the first anti-war novels to appear during the war itself, and remains one of the most powerful. In the novels set in the febrile years of the 1920s Macaulay experimented formally with structure and voice, and explored, or played with, the themes that came to be associated with the modernist movement, that is, notions of time, identity and consciousness; these novels, which include *Dangerous Ages* (1921), *Told by an Idiot* (1923), *Orphan Island* (1924), *Crewe Train* (1926), and *Keeping Up Appearances* (1928), were a huge commercial success.

In the 1930s Rose Macaulay turned to history and biography, with an acclaimed historical novel, *They Were Defeated* (1932), set in the seventeenth-century; a book on John Milton came out in 1934. Her explorations of the past became a way of understanding the restless times she lived in, and also a way of understanding her own restless, divided self. Throughout her life, in her written journalism and her radio work, she was a sharp and vigorous commentator on matters of public and popular interest. She was always an intrepid traveller and in the 1940s and 1950s she became a stylish and engaging travel writer. After ten years silence as a novelist she returned triumphantly to fiction in 1950, publishing first *The World My Wilderness* (1950), set in a ruined London after the Blitz, and, six years later, her final book, *The Towers of Trebizond* (1956).

In 1918 Rose Macaulay, working in the Ministry of Information, met an ex-priest turned novelist called Gerald O'Donovan. O'Donovan's first novel, *Father Ralph*, an autobiographical novel about an idealistic young priest in turn-of-the-century Galway, had been published in 1913. When he and Rose met he had been married for eight years, and his wife, Beryl, was about to give birth to their third child.

Did he conceal from Rose the fact that he was married and the father of young children? Possibly. Rose set up such a scenario in her 1923 novel *Told by an Idiot*; her protagonist Rome Garden is already caught in the coils of love when she learns that her lover has a wife and family. Jean Macaulay, Rose's younger sister, firmly believed that O'Donovan delayed telling Rose; but she and Margaret (the oldest Macaulay sibling) were anyway predisposed to blame O'Donovan for the affair. All three sisters were devout church-goers (Margaret would later become a nun); all three saw adultery as a sin. By continuing the affair Rose would be choosing to place herself outside the church in which she had grown up.

Probably both Rose and Gerald struggled against the inevitable. Gerald's temporary removal of self and family to Italy in 1920 suggests that he made such an effort.

But in 1921 a choice was made. The price that Rose paid was not only her spiritual life within the Anglican communion, but also the sustaining intimacy which – despite the differences in their lifestyles – she had long enjoyed with her sisters Margaret and Jean. They viewed her choice as 'a sad tragedy' (Jean Macaulay, 18 August 1960, ERM Box 4). But for her life as a writer it proved a price worth paying. Her affair with Gerald O'Donovan gave her love without dependence and, crucially, no burden of domestic responsibility.

A pattern was established that allowed Rose into Gerald's home life: throughout the 1920s and 30s she would have lunch every other Sunday at the O'Donovan family table in their house in Surrey. She became an honorary aunt to the three children. This arrangement suited both Rose and Gerald, and one can only hope that welcoming Rose into the family afforded Gerald's wife, Beryl, a sense that she was at least partly in control. Whatever game was played out in the O'Donovan household, in order to spend time alone without subterfuge Rose and Gerald frequently travelled together abroad. In the 1920s and 1930s Rose was travelling regularly, sometimes holidaying with friends, sometimes on a newspaper assignment or other job – she was a co-lecturer with Gustav Holst on a Lunn tour in Switzerland in 1925 – and would simply stay abroad at the end of her trip and meet up with Gerald.

Gerald made no excuses to his family for his frequent disappearances. He had brought up his children in the belief that the savage representation of Irish Catholicism in his novels made him a target for the ire of the powerful Catholic establishment, and that his family should never know where he was or what he was doing for fear one of them might 'let it out'.

Years later the publisher Victor Gollancz referred to the love affair between Rose and Gerald as 'one of the best-kept secrets in London' (Gollancz 1968, 83).

><>

After leaving Ireland in the early 1900s Gerald was forever haunted by a feeling of unbelonging. Just as his desire for secrecy spoke to Rose's passionate privacy, so his outsiderness offered a reflection for hers: outside the mainstream, outside the literary establishment, outside gazing in, like Laurie in Rose's last novel gazing at the towers of Trebizond shimmering in the distance. For Rose Macaulay it was a creative place to inhabit. Her role as a writer, as an observer of rather than as a participant in the tale told by an idiot, was mirrored in her personal life. The dangers that marriage poses to women's creativity is a theme that recurs in Rose's inter-war novels; through a variety of characters and settings she shows us how the imagination is stifled by domestic responsibility.

Considering the secrecy with which they guarded their relationship it is perhaps unsurprising that Gerald O'Donovan seems most present in Rose Macaulay's work when he is absent and she is mourning his loss. He is painfully present in 'Miss Anstruther's Letters', a short story written in 1941 soon after Rose's London flat was hit in a bombing raid. In the story Miss Anstruther's lover is recently dead. So raw is Miss Anstruther's grief that she has been unable yet to reread the letters he has sent her over the years; she has been saving them up for a time when she can read them without giving way to despair. Her flat takes a direct hit, and only one scrap of paper escapes the consuming fire: written on it is one hurtful phrase that turns all the years of passion and love into 'a drift of grey ashes' like the remains of the letters themselves. Miss Anstruther herself becomes 'a drifting ghost' (Macaulay 2019, 282). When Rose Macaulay wrote the story, Gerald O'Donovan, whose letters had been destroyed in the wreckage of her flat, was not yet dead, but he was dying. The written record of the love that had flourished during what is described in this heart-breaking story as the 'secret stolen travels of twenty years' would never be replaced (Macaulay 2019, 280).

When Rose Macaulay died in 1958 she left no journals, but three volumes of her letters, edited by Constance Babington Smith, were published a few years later. These volumes did little to enhance Rose's posthumous literary reputation, and exercised a pernicious influence on the reception of Constance Babington Smith's 1972 biography, and even on the reception of the later biography by Jane Emery, published in 1991, which provided a solid and serious literary appraisal of Rose Macaulay's life and work. Two volumes of the letters (*Letters to a Friend from Rose Macaulay, 1950-1952,* in 1961, and *Last Letters to a Friend from Rose Macaulay, 1952-1958*, in 1962) consist of Rose's correspondence, which she initiated in 1950, with Father Hamilton Johnson of the Anglican order the Cowley Fathers. Rose had left the church in the early 1920s, when she had embarked on her love affair with the married O'Donovan. Through her correspondence with Hamilton Johnson she found a route back into the Anglican church. These letters were redacted by Constance Babington Smith before publication, and she placed the originals in the Macaulay archive in Trinity College, Cambridge, with a fifty-year embargo.

The third volume (*Letters to a Sister from Rose Macaulay,* 1964) contains letters from Rose to her younger sister Jean. Although they cover a much longer period than the correspondence with Hamilton Johnson, gaps and silences shout their presence. Jean was a devout Anglican who had never questioned her faith. She didn't approve of Rose's affair with Gerald; if it was ever referred to in their correspondence (which it may well not have been) those references were deleted. Jean on her own admission had slashed and burned her way through the letters before she handed them over to Constance Babington Smith to edit for publication, leaving an anodyne compilation that in subject matter was weighted towards the church concerns that interested Jean herself.

Constance Babington Smith was a distant cousin of the Macaulays who had first met Rose in the 1950s, when Rose's religious feelings were once again finding expression. She regretted the extent of Jean's censoring. But she shared Jean's desire that Rose's letters to Father Hamilton Johnson should tell a particular story: that of Rose's remorse for her sinful relationship, and her joyful return to the church from the self-imposed exile she had chosen a quarter of a century earlier.

In the Epilogue I give an account of the contentious reception accorded these three volumes of letters.

A fourth volume of Rose Macaulay's letters (*Dearest Jean: Rose Macaulay's Letters to a Cousin*), written to her cousin Jean Smith, edited by Jean Smith's nephew Martin Ferguson Smith, was published in 2011.

To my knowledge none of Rose's letters to Gerald O'Donovan have survived.

><>

A woman of contradictions and complexities, Rose Macaulay was gregarious but intensely private, warm-hearted but secretive, sharp-tongued but easily provoked to laughter, highly intellectual but retaining a delight in childlike physical activity, passionate about literature but constantly mocking and satirising those caught up in literary endeavour. She gave the impression of being sexually uninterested in men ('Poor dear Rose, judging from her works, is a Eunuch', wrote Virginia Woolf to Hope Mirrlees [Nicolson and Trautmann eds 1980, 497], who did not take kindly to her own books being less popular than Rose's), while for a quarter of a century she was passionately and, according to her own criteria, sinfully, in love with a married man. The relationship ended only with his death in 1942. When Daisy, in the 1928 novel *Keeping Up Appearances*, reflects on people's 'queer hidden selves', she could be thinking about Rose Macaulay herself (Macaulay 1928, 153).

I was originally attracted to Rose by the 'queer hidden selves' of her writing life, the way her fiction coexists with biography and travel, her scholarly sobriety with a light-hearted playfulness. I was also attracted by the secrets in her own life. I was interested by the way that she was able to so organise the life of her heart that her love affair was protected and she herself was free to write. It seems to me not easy for a woman to carve out for herself the emotional space within which she can pursue her art without sacrificing love or friendships.

The journal I kept while researching and writing my biography of Rose Macaulay charts the changes in my relationship with her over that period of intense obsessive thinking and dreaming, from 1998 to the end of 2002. It also records my encounters with a number of other people – in the flesh and on the page – whom I met in the course of my pursuit of the person I came to see as 'my' Rose.

When I started my research I was living (and still live) in North Somerset, about ten miles from Bristol. My three children were teenagers – the eldest turned 18 in 2001 – and for the previous seven years, since leaving The Women's Press in 1991 after more than a decade as general editor, and founding editor of the science fiction list, I had picked up bits and pieces of freelance work from various kindly publishers, radio producers and department heads. I was editing anthologies, abridging books for BBC Radio 4, teaching extra-mural classes at Bristol University. As I record in the following pages, soon after I began my research on Rose Macaulay I was offered the job of presenting Radio 4's *A Good Read*, a weekly programme in which the presenter and her two guests choose and discuss a favourite paperback. It was what amounted to a proper job, properly paid; unfortunately it turned out to be short-lived. I returned to my varied freelance life, and in 2001 I won a wonderfully confidence-boosting Arts Council award for the work I was doing on Rose Macaulay.

The journal ends with my picking up the threads of my relationship with Rose ten years after I had finished work on the biography, when the embargo placed by Constance Babington Smith on the original copies of Rose's letters to Father Hamilton Johnson was finally lifted.

Sarah LeFanu, 2021

Chapter One: Beginnings, 1998

First lesson for the novice biographer: don't assume when you're reading about people living forty or fifty years ago that they are necessarily dead. Second lesson: don't assume that they are going to be around for you to interview at your leisure in a year or two's time. Talk to them now.

Constance Babington Smith published her editions of Rose Macaulay's letters to Father Hamilton Johnson, and Rose's letters to her sister Jean, in the early 1960s, soon after Rose died. Constance was then aged about fifty. 'Is Constance still around?' asked Jean and Richard Gooder, who were kindly putting me up for a couple of nights in June 1998 while I did some very preliminary digging in the Rose Macaulay archives in Trinity College for a proposal for a new biography of Rose. Constance, who settled in Cambridge at the end of the war, had donated to Trinity's Wren Library all of her research papers on the editions of Rose's letters, and on her own 1972 biography of Rose, along with the Macaulay family papers that she had been bequeathed on Jean Macaulay's death.

'Oh, I doubt it,' I replied. 'She'd be ancient if she was still alive.'

Richard grabbed the telephone directory. 'Well, let's just have a look.

And there she was, Constance Babington Smith, 4 Little St Mary's Lane. Barely five minutes' walk from the Gooders' house.

'Why don't you give her a ring?' said Richard.

The profession of biography, like journalism, demands that you overcome your natural shyness about approaching strangers and asking them to give up their time to answer your questions. I didn't ring up Constance that evening. My nerve failed me. And anyway Tony Tanner came round to discuss with Richard the marking of the American Literature paper, and we all drank daiquiris and gossiped about people in the English Faculty. Tony Tanner, so crippled he could only just manage to walk with the aid of two sticks, was sadly changed from the dark-haired dashing man I had a crush on when I was twenty and reading out to him my undergraduate essays on Mark Twain; but still clever, attractive, and full of charm.

I wrote to Constance as soon as I got home. She said she would be delighted to talk to me, but warned me that a recent stroke had impaired her speech. At the end of September 1998 I met her for the first time and recorded our conversation; as a result of the stroke she would pause every so often in the middle of a sentence, and ask me to remind her what it was she'd been saying. 'You must get writing!' she urged me. Over the next six months I worked on my proposal and had the biography commissioned by Virago, and at the same time recorded my first series as presenter of BBC Radio 4's paperback programme, *A Good Read*.

My original Rose-proposal had been modelled on Richard Holmes' pursuit of Robert Louis Stevenson through the Cevennes, which he wrote about in *Footsteps: Adventures of a Romantic Biographer*. I wanted to follow in the footsteps of Rose Macaulay when she drove down the coast of Spain in 1946, a journey that she wrote up and published as *Fabled Shore*. The book records the ghostly voices she hears from the distant past: Carthaginians, Greeks, Moors, nineteenth-century English merchants and their families. She travels through a landscape depopulated by civil war, carrying inside her a burden of secret grief. She had been grieving for four years, ever since the death of her lover Gerald O'Donovan.

This proposal attracted no interest whatsoever from any publisher but I turned it into a drama proposal that was accepted by Radio 4. I then found myself working simultaneously on two periods in Rose Macaulay's life separated by fifty years or so, and in two different forms: one form shaped by documents, correspondence, the visible traces of a life, and the other demanding a narrative of imagined conversations and interior monologues.

Early in 1999 Constance had another, very debilitating, stroke. When I returned to Cambridge in April I found her – tiny, frail and almost speechless – in a geriatric ward; from there she moved to a nursing home, where she stayed until her death in the summer of 2000.

At our first meeting in Little St Mary's Lane Constance grumbled that Jean Macaulay had cut and burned her way through all her sister's letters before Constance had had a chance to read them in their entirety. And then she tantalised me with: 'Do you think Rose should have ...?' Should have what? She was unable to finish the sentence, so I never found out.

I wish I had had the nerve, or the foresight, or the simple sense to ring her that evening in June 1998 and settle myself on her doorstep until I had asked her everything that I could possibly think to ask.

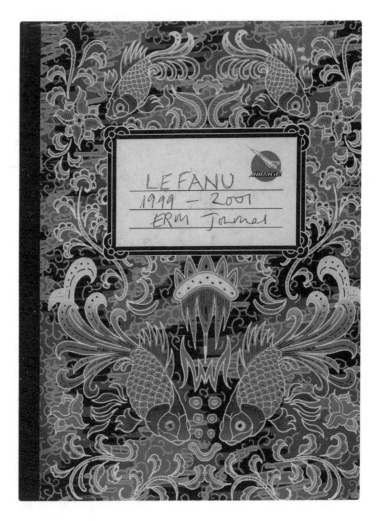

1. Cover of writing journal with fishes.

Chapter Two: May–December 1999

Home/Cambridge/Home

26 May: Home

In Allsorts Discount Hardware Store in Nailsea I found a hardback notebook, made in Indonesia, decorated with four multi-coloured carp – orange, green, blue, purple, yellow – with flamboyantly foliate tails swimming through an intricately patterned underwater seaweed world. Only 59p. It strikes me as obvious and necessary that I dedicate it to my Rose Macaulay work, the biography and the play – currently called *Her Mermaid Self* – and fill it with my floating thoughts on a woman who called herself 'vaguely ichthyous and mer' and who imagined one of her clergyman forebears, a rector in Devon perhaps, falling in love with a mermaid thrown by the waves onto the sandy beach ...

This evening I finished James Lees-Milne's entertainingly bitchy *Ancestral Voices*. In his entry for 27 July 1943 he describes Rose Macaulay as 'dry and twitchy' at a dinner party where they were both guests. I know that it was the first anniversary of Gerald O'Donovan's funeral. But how was Lees-Milne to know? According to Victor Gollancz Rose's affair with Gerald had been 'the best-kept secret in London'.

7 August

I'm working on the first draft of the play, no longer called *Her Mermaid Self* but, at Felicity the producer's suggestion, *Thin Woman in a Morris Minor*. I've structured it around alternating scenes of swimming and driving: two of Rose's three favourite occupations, the third being talking, but not now, not in the dry years of her grief for Gerald. And in between the swimming and driving scenes – or, as I hope, cunningly interwoven – the letters she writes to him that she'll never post. The radio audience (those who don't know Rose's story) won't know until towards the end that he's already dead.

But this month I am having to record one programme per week of *A Good Read*. John Sutherland has chosen *Midnight's Children*, which is a week's work in itself just to read (this is his second choice; the BBC, running scared, won't allow us to discuss his first choice, *The Satanic Verses*). I'm having to snatch at *Thin Woman* moments; not the easiest way to write.

><

15 September

From *What Not*, Rose's weird 1918 falling-in-love-with-Gerald *roman à clef*: 'Many persons have been called upon, for one cause or another, to wait in nervous anticipation hour by hour for the signal which shall herald their own destruction' (Macaulay 1918, 155). As I await, now, the call from one of the Radio 4 executive producers, Fiona or Elizabeth, to tell me that I have been booted from the presenter's chair of *A Good Read*. My friend Sara Davies, who is the programme producer, warned me on Sunday night to expect it. She had heard that big chief James Boyle thinks my accent too posh for his Radio 4. For two days my stomach has lurched with sick dread every time the phone rings.

><

21 September

Newnham College, Cambridge. I've been given a room in Strachey – I remember these rooms from 25 years ago as being enviably freshly-painted, and boasting built-in cupboards containing washbasin and mirror, so you didn't have to trail the dark corridors in your dressing-gown as we had to in Clough. But now the basin tap rattles loose in its socket, and the walls are pocked with pinholes and the grey greasy spots left by blu-tack. £16 per night.

I spent all morning in the Wren Library in Trinity reading the correspondence between Jean Macaulay and Constance Babington Smith. I had been prejudiced against Jean because of what Constance had said about her radical revision of her sister's letters after Rose died; she particularly edited out Rose's disrespectful comments on priests and clergymen and her jokes about churches high and low. I imagine Jean's anxiety when Constance got in touch about bringing out an edition of Rose's letters to Father Hamilton Johnson. So much to hide! Would she be able to trust Constance?

Jean's first letters to Constance are polite but wary; then a friendship develops between the two women, a friendship that's strengthened by the furore that erupts in the press, taking both women utterly by surprise, when *Letters to a Friend* is published. The furore: Should the letters have been published at all? If not, who was to blame? Hamilton Johnson the recipient, or Constance Babington Smith and Jean Macaulay, the executors? Surely Hamilton Johnson was under the oath of the confessional? Was Hamilton Johnson even a real priest? Who had betrayed whom? And so on. (See Epilogue.)

The last time I was here I read a copy (I assume made by Constance) of a letter from Rose to her cousin Dorothea Conybeare, dated two days before Rose's death in 1958, in which she attempts to justify the horrid behaviour of 'the Five' towards their baby sister Eleanor, when they were children running wild by the sea in Varazze, in the 1880s and 90s. Rose justifies their meanness by saying that Eleanor was such an unattractive child the older siblings couldn't help but be repelled by her. Is this credible? Eleanor, aged four or five, was apparently 'greedy' for jam; is this enough to make her brothers and sisters find her 'unattractive'? Would a ten-year-old even think in such terms? Or, more likely, did the older children take their cue from their mother Grace, who never hid her dislike of her youngest child, always comparing her unfavourably to the golden-haired Gertrude, who had died of meningitis aged three-and-a-half? For Rose to be writing about this seventy years later suggests profound feelings of guilt and unease. But it's not the full letter, so it is difficult to make a judgement. Was the original (of which there is no sign) cut by Jean, or did Constance edit as she transcribed; or were deletions made in turn by each of them? Both women were keen to tidy up Rose in posthumous print.

The scholars' table in the Wren Library is way down at the southern end, hidden from the doorway behind a large white marble statue of Lord Byron in loose cravat and fitted flared coat. You nod hello to the librarian on duty at the door, then walk the length of the library to take your place at the table, where you sit with the other readers under the eye of another librarian. There are seventeen or eighteen Rose Macaulay boxes. The one that contains Rose's letters to Hamilton Johnson is sealed until 12 June 2012. You can order up two or three boxes at a time, which are placed on a bench to one side of the table, and then the supervisor hands you the items from within – notebook, packet of photos, whatever – one at a time. When I was here for the first time last year I was surprised by how much of the correspondence was not in original manuscript form, but consisted of copies transcribed by Constance Babington Smith. Curious, I asked one of the archivists, a cheery fellow I found sitting at a computer in one of the alcoves, surrounded by teetering piles of ancient calfbound volumes in Latin and Greek: 'Would it be possible to tell whether the material in the sealed box is original material or copies?' 'Sure,' he said. 'I'll go and have a look. Any excuse to dig around where I'm not meant to.' He returned three-quarters of an hour later with the answer: originals; and left me pondering the precise meaning of the word 'sealed'.

It feels extraordinarily privileged and is extraordinarily pleasurable to sit in silence all day in a beautiful library turning over the pages of old diaries and letters. The solitary nature of scholarship and research … 'She travels fastest who travels alone,' wrote Mary Beard, adapting Kipling, in the *London Review of Books*. She was reviewing a biography of Nobel Prize-winning Dorothy Hodgkin, which, Mary Beard said, failed to mention that Dorothy Hodgkin's husband and children, far from constituting the close and happy family described in the popular press, were in fact ruthlessly sidelined. I have a dim memory of a Hodgkin daughter being involved in Vietnam, and possibly the Communist Party and Medical Aid – 70s anti-war stuff anyway. I don't travel alone, and am very pleased that I don't, and will certainly never win the Nobel Prize – but the pleasure of being able to concentrate on one's own work for days at a time is exquisite.

I left the Wren in the early afternoon and walked over the Backs and up Castle Hill to the County Records Office where I read Rose's uncle Edward Conybeare's 1880s and 1890s diaries, in which he records every addition to the Macaulay household and the varying state of health and mind of his adored and spoiled younger sister, Rose's mother, Grace. Each page of the pocket-sized diaries is crammed with his tiny neat hand.

I haven't yet received my marching orders from *A Good Read*. I hear from Sara that Boyle can't make up his mind.

><>

23 September: Cambridge. I woke up with a sore throat. 'Bad throat' is a recurring phrase in Grace Macaulay's diaries of the 1880s and 1890s, sometimes followed by 'stayed in bed all day', or more frequently 'breakfasted in bed'. Reading all these diaries – Grace's and her brother Edward Conybeare's – makes me feel it really is worthwhile to keep a regular, properly dated diary. Edward, too, often suffers a 'bad throat', or a 'cruel cough'. The details of a hundred years ago – the ponies, the presents, the family trips, the meals – spring vividly from the page. George Macaulay's new Jaeger nightshirt was stolen in Naples. He fell asleep on the train and missed Varazze; he had to walk home from the next village through the pitch-dark countryside.

❧

24 September: Cambridge

Throat worse. Knives slice through it when I try to speak. And I'm still awaiting the chop from *A Good Read*.

I felt I must do something, something active to allay my anxiety. I drove the few miles out to Great Shelford to see if I could find Southernwood, the Macaulay family home from 1906 to 1917. It was easy: the name was on the gate, so I left the car on the main road and walked down the tree-lined drive, and boldly rang the bell on the door, which was opened by a middle-aged woman who knew immediately what I was talking about when I said the name Macaulay. Could I take some photos of the house, I asked? I must warn my mother, she said. I had a picture in my head of an old lady resting in the garden beneath a plaid travelling rug. But no, her mother, although tiny with age, was hard at work in the flowerbeds with trowel, fork and spade. The house is squarely solid, its plainness offset by a castellated quasi-tower on the west side, and large bas reliefs, of a pot of flowers, and a swag of foliage, set into the stonework. Built in 1898, said Mrs B, the owner. She told me that the willows by the gate had been planted by Rose's mother Grace from slips taken from her brother Edward Conybeare's vicarage at Barrington, a few miles west of Great Shelford, where Grace had spent so much time as a girl. Did I know someone called Jonathan Hunt, she asked, an expert on the Conybeares? No, I said. Apparently he works at the Fitzwilliam. A curator? I asked. No, she didn't think so. A janitor or attendant, she thinks. He's read and transcribed all or most of Edward Conybeare's diaries. Mrs B was apologetic about not showing me round the inside of the house, but she had to get the supper ready. I said of course of course, I wasn't expecting to ring on the doorbell and be invited inside. She said to phone next time I'm in Cambridge, and visit them again. But just quickly before I go I must admire the original red and black marble tessellated hall floor, and – and here she lifted up the door mat – the matching mat well. It was beautiful.

><

28 September

Home. I'm convinced there's more to Rose Macaulay/Rupert Brooke than has ever appeared in print. Rose was a writer and a contemporary of his, a family friend and daughter of his one-time tutor. I think the Macaulays saw more of Rupert's elder brother Dick, who died of alcoholism in his twenties, but even so, why is Rose so little mentioned in the Brooke literature? Brooke must have read the novels of hers that came out while she was living in Great Shelford. He was living just down the road, in Grantchester. Her fourth novel, *The Valley Captives*, was published in 1911. Which month? Brooke moved into The Old Vicarage in May.

><

4 October

At last, it's happened. It was Fiona who pulled the short straw to ring me up and tell me that Boyle wanted rid of me. Fiona is a nice enough woman. He's looking to use more diverse voices, perhaps a black presenter, she explained. Oh well, that's all right then isn't it? I could feel my throat closing up as I listened to her soft Scottish burr; could barely squeeze out OK, yeah, bye.

><

18 October

I received a lovely letter from Philippa Pearce, who grew up in the old flour mill on the Cam in Great Shelford, the King's Mill, where her father, and before him her grandfather, were millers. Her grandparents and parents didn't 'know' the Macaulays because of rigid social distinctions in the village. The Pearces were Chapel.

22 October

I thought I'd come to terms with losing *A Good Read*, and thank God the waiting is over, so my stomach no longer lurches every time the phone rings, but I'm continuing to dream, night after night after night, about being sacked – and receiving the news in crowded train carriages, in tiny rooms, or standing on the pavement outside a house. Or, that I'm invited on to someone else's programme but when I turn up I find the studio door's locked and I'm left hammering on the outside of it to be let in. Or, that I'm in the studio and the green light comes on but I can't speak – that I have cancer of the throat. Last night's dream even involved ghastly stuff about the break-up of The Women's Press. That was nearly ten years ago, and I thought I had got over it. But it must still be swirling around in the unconscious.

2 November

I've heard that three women are lined up to take over and share the *A Good Read* presenter's role, two of whom have recently appeared as my guests on the programme. When Ros de Lanerolle was sacked from The Women's Press, seven of us resigned in solidarity. But that was a decade ago. Obviously it is every woman for herself now.

11 November

Yesterday I started to write about Grace Macaulay beginning to have babies. I wrote about the way you suddenly become quite a different person from the person you were before, how you become ruled by your body and how you become subject to the demands of another, separate, being.

This morning I heard from Rowena Fowler (my boss, Head of

Continuing Education in the English Department at Bristol University, and in charge of the Creative Writing Diploma), whom I had asked to check out for me, in the online academic journals that I am not able to access, the title of the Mary Kingsley novel which Edward Conybeare refers to and which I think might have been published in 1885. (Mary Kingsley was the daughter of Charles 'Water Babies' Kingsley, and a cousin of the other, intrepid, Mary Kingsley, who wrote *Travels in West Africa* and died of typhoid while nursing Boer prisoners of war in South Africa.) Rowena told me that Kingsley's *Colonel Enderby's Wife* was published that year. Might this be the novel Edward Conybeare means, saying it includes 'cruel' (a favourite word of his) portraits of his sister Grace and his wife Frances? Rowena tells me it's in three volumes. Apparently it was a popular success and was translated into Polish. I'll order it through the wonderful inter-library loan: 50p for any obscure book you want.

Ian Lightbody, from Liverpool College, has sent me some stuff on Rose's grandfather, Grace's father, Reverend William J Conybeare, who was the first principal of the school (then Liverpool Collegiate Institution) in the 1840s. He had a glass eye – the result of a fight when he was a schoolboy at Westminster and a boy chucked a stone at him. Later he wrote a novel – another triple-decker, what stamina they had then – called *Perversion: or the Causes and Consequences of Infidelity*.

><>

14 November

I have found out that a flight to Genoa costs £140.00, which I can afford with the help of the travel grant from the Society of Authors. Varazze – Rose's childhood paradise – is half an hour by train down the coast. I'd like to be there for the Feast of Santa Caterina on 30 April to see if the Varazzians still sing their hymn to St Catherine, *Difendi, O Caterina/ da guerra e terremoto/ Il popol di Varazze/ A te devoto* (Protect, O Catherine, from war and earthquake, your devotees, the people of Varazze), as they process along the shoreline on her name day. Rose describes 'the Five' – herself, Margaret, Jean, Aulay and Will – in their sailor frocks and sailor suits, following the procession through the narrow *carrugi* of Varazze down to the sea and along to the Church of St Catherine. The hymn was inscribed on Rose's heart. She wrote it into at least three of her – pre-1914 – novels. The young Crevequers sing it in *The Furnace* as they play on the sand in front of the square red house (itself a portrait of Villa Levante, or Villa Macolai as it was known locally during the years when the Macaulays lived there), and again as they row out to sea in *Views and Vagabonds*. In *The Lee Shore* Peter Margerison hums *Difendi, O Caterina,* … to himself as he wanders up and down the Ligurian coast from Varazze to Cogoleto, with his baby and a donkey-drawn cart.

><>

18 November

Very cold, or as Edward Conybeare might say, cruel cold. My fingers are numb after tapping on the keyboard for three hours. I've finished the first draft of the first chapter: 'Grace and George'. How complicated they both were. A tattered and torn copy of Rose's 1919 poetry collection *Three Days* has arrived from the British Library via inter-library loan.

><>

19 November

I discovered from Teresa Whistler's biography of Walter de la Mare that Rupert Brooke made out his will leaving his royalties to Walter de la Mare and two other poets – so that they could devote themselves to writing good poetry and not waste their energies in hack work to pay the bills and support their numerous children. What an extraordinarily generous gift. And of course within ten years after his death Rupert had become hugely famous and the income was substantial. Rupert's mother thought this was a wonderful thing to do, as well. All three of her sons died when they were barely adult men. Her only daughter had died in infancy. How unimaginably terrible.

><>

24 November

Yesterday I went to Clifton College, where Aulay was sent to be schooled. In these public (so-called) schools the very buildings reek of privilege. I felt unsettled by unhappy memories of my own boarding school days. In Aulay's old House I met the current housemaster, who was friendly, plump and cricket-obsessed, and his amiable wife in calf-length kilt. Their cordiality reminded me of how I used to dislike that false-home feeling. I always preferred the honest chilly gloom of the main school buildings to the fake homeliness of the House. Virginia Woolf's brother Thoby was miserable at Clifton a year or two after Aulay.

2 December

I had a meeting yesterday at the BBC with Jeremy Howe, who has been appointed script editor of *Thin Woman in a Morris Minor*. He pulled my draft apart. Strange underwater dreams last night.

16 December

I had just settled down to work yesterday, picking up the threads of *Thin Woman* from where I had left them last week, when I was startled by the clanging of the front door bell, which nobody ever uses as everyone comes in through the kitchen door and shouts if they can't see us. I found Mrs NextDoor on the doorstep. I invited her in but she refused with a toss of her big hair and without warning launched into a screaming tirade against us, shouting at me that we must do something to stop the rainwater flooding their drive. I remember how our next door neighbour in Bristol accused us of poisoning the toads in his garden. He had a heart attack soon after. I know these accusations are crazy – what can I do about the amount of rain we've been having (or the fact that Jeff's toads were dying)? Nonetheless I feel shaken and upset by the noise and the anger.

Rose's 1914 poetry collection *The Two Blind Countries* arrived through inter-library loan from Sussex University, donated to them from the library of G K A Bell, Bishop of Chichester 1929-58 and his widow. It came with all the usual bits and pieces of paper clipped onto the title page, including a slip saying 'For use in the library only', and then, handwritten, 'unless reader known to be very reliable', against which someone has pencilled a big tick. A reliable reader: a judgment to be proud of.

Chapter Three: January–April 2000

Home/London/Rugby/Oxford/Home

19 January: Home

Ghosts, shadows and vague shapes glimpsed through veils – first cousins to Walter de la Mare's wraiths and spirits – flit through the poems in *The Two Blind Countries*.

I had to drop *Thin Woman in a Morris Minor* over Christmas and the New Year but once the children were back at school I managed to finish the second draft in ten days. I have thickened it up with more about Gerald O'Donovan's past: that is, with how Rose imagines his past, or rather how I imagine she imagines his past. As Rose steps into the cathedral in Valencia I have made her wonder about Gerald's early days as a priest in Loughrea. And I have put in a scene where she remembers their first meeting – in the Ministry of Information, when she's huddled in a greatcoat against the chilliness of the 1918 spring – when he failed to tell her he was married. Writing the play gives me licence to make things up: thoughts, feelings, conversations.

The BBC producer rang on Monday. She's been ill, so the contract hasn't gone through. I desperately need some money to pay off the Christmas debts.

✄

22 January

I had a cyst on my chin removed last week. At the school governors' meeting on Wednesday three of the women there, noticing the butterfly tapes, individually and discreetly took me aside and showed me, to encourage me, their own old facial scars, now barely visible: one from a mole removal, one something to do with cancer, and the third from a cyst like mine. I don't think that any of them was aware that the others had had facial surgery; each one was offering me the gift of a secret of their own.

✄

1 February

What a terrible struggle. I thought I had finished *Thin Woman*, but Jeremy Howe has torn it to pieces once again and now I am wrestling to weave the tattered shreds of it back together. I have lost all sense of the order in which things happen, and of the order in which they're dramatically revealed. It all seems *arbitrary*.

7 February

Finished *Colonel Enderby's Wife*. Mary Kingsley wrote under the pleasing name of Lucas Malet. I couldn't find in it any 'cruel portraits' of Grace Macaulay and Frances Conybeare. Was Edward Conybeare being paranoid? Or have I perhaps misread or misunderstood his reference?

Wednesday 9 February

The Little Innocents childhood anthology arrived from Southampton Library via inter-library loan. Rose writes about the 'square red house' in Varazze and the doings of 'the Five'. (In *Colonel Enderby's Wife* the widow Pierce-Dawnay inhabits a red villa in 'Terzia', just down the coast from Genoa. Was this what made uncle Edward think Mary Kingsley was writing about Grace?) *Little Innocents* also includes John Betjeman on bullying at Marlborough in the 1920s (an experience revisited in *Summoned by Bells*). And Nina Hamnett on what she wore as a little girl in the eighteen-nineties: thick black stockings, buttoned boots, heavy cotton pinnies etc. At the age of four she was forced into black woollen stockings because her grandmother thought that socks were 'indecent'.

Bad day on Monday: depths of despair. Can't write, not earning any money, will never finish the biography. To London tonight to spend tomorrow in the British Library to look at the Rose Macaulay and Rupert Brooke poems in the *Saturday Westminster* competitions. I looked at Nigel Jones's new biography of Rupert Brooke when I was in Blackwell's yesterday, and found only one reference to Rose, that she 'nursed secret romantic feelings for Rupert Brooke, apparent in her early novels.' I think not!

26 February: London

Well, Rose was getting her poems printed in the *Saturday Westminster* for two years, 1905 and 1906, before Rupert Brooke ever appeared in its pages.

I couldn't resist ordering up Rose's grandfather W J Conybeare's *Perversion* – all three volumes – and raced through it. By the end my eyeballs were spinning. It begins compellingly, with some vivid descriptions of young boys being horribly bullied at a public school: Charles and Sapper are forced to sit side by side and smoke cigars until they vomit; they have the red hot cigar ends pressed into their cheeks; they're strung up by their thumbs and flogged with brambles; forced to dance naked in front of the older boys; made to eat tallow candles and wash them down with dirty water from the washbasins. Rose surely drew on these scenes for the sufferings of Tudor Vallon in *The Valley Captives*, published 1911. The next two volumes of *Perversion* digress into the dangers of Mormonism, Tractarianism and atheism.

The Humanities reading rooms in the British Library – especially the lower one – are depressingly gloomy. Why weren't they designed to let in more natural light?

I went on to John Murray's handsome Georgian building at 50 Albemarle Street to look at the files on Rose's early novels, and sat in the room where Rose would have met John Murray in 1906 after he had accepted her first novel *Abbots Verney*. It is famous as the room where more famous writers than Rose – Charles Darwin, Lord Byron, Walter Scott (Jane Austen? No, I think they conducted business by post) conversed with earlier John Murrays. It was in this room that the pages of Lord Byron's memoirs were fed unread to the fire in the marble fireplace, only three days after Byron's death. Ian Hamilton, in his brilliant book about literary estates and the awful things that executors get up to, writes of the 'suspicious swiftness' with which Byron's executor Hobhouse acted.

Glnny Murray was incredibly kind. She brought me a cup of tea, and went off searching for more material, turning up a letter from George Macaulay to John Murray, asking him to look at a story by another of his daughters. Margaret? I guess so. What story?

She, Ginny Murray, told me that her father-in-law John Murray VI (I think) had been born there, in the house, and had had his appendix out 'on that very table'.

Why are Rose's letters so diffident? They're all: 'I'm sure you'll find the book too ... ...' Boring, short, lacking in wide appeal: a whole range of negative epithets. And each time John Murray courteously replies, in elegant script, 'Dear Miss Macaulay, we would be honoured to publish your book ...' Was she made nervous by publication? Yet it would have been so easy *not* to be published. In a way I sympathise: I recognise that desire to pre-empt potential critics. But at the same time I feel exasperated. Pull yourself together, Rose; John Murray *wants* to publish you. Count yourself lucky!

In *The Secret River* file I found desperate telegrams from Rose in Great Shelford on the discovery that the dedication 'To my mother' had been omitted from the printed copies; news of Aulay's violent death in India – news from which Grace never fully recovered – had been received only a few days beforehand, making the mistake even more egregious. Rose's tone is accusatory against John Murray, although the correspondence suggests the oversight was as much her fault as his. Yet my copy of the novel – the copy given by Rose to her sister Jean on publication, which Jean gave to Constance and which Constance gave to me – includes the dedication. It is a beautiful cloth edition with four blue flowers one above the other on the front, each growing horizontally out of the green foliage that twines up the spine. In 1909 Rose's books were still being published under the name R Macaulay. Perhaps John Murray was able to halt the print run and have the omission rectified?

Later I went to see Almodóvar's film *All About my Mother*. I started crying at the very beginning, when the poor woman's 17-year-old son dies; then carried on crying as I watched, amidst Almodóvar's panorama of transvestites, junkies and hookers, a woman dying in childbirth, a father dying of AIDS, and an old man losing his mind. I felt in need of a large drink afterwards.

><

27 February

Home. When I looked more closely at the dedication 'To my mother' in my copy of *The Secret River*, I saw that it seems to have been stamped or pressed, rather than printed, onto the prelim page; you can feel the indentation between your fingertips.

In London I met up for a drink with Caroline, with whom I had been at the convent of the Holy Child in the mid-1960s. One of her elder brothers, whom I remember as predatory when I was thirteen and staying with them in the holidays, but who in the intervening years had turned into a respectable father-of-four, had died of a heart attack ten days earlier. His turned out to be the first in a series of deaths I heard about as soon as I got home: my old friend Mon (Monica) McLean told me her daughter's boyfriend had been found dead in a hotel room in Beijing. My sister-in-law Juliet's father, Noel Annan, for whom Rose Macaulay was, as he put it, the fox that he started in pursuit of 'The Intellectual Aristocracy', the closely-woven web of nineteenth-century British intellectuals that included Macaulays, Darwins and Huxleys, died a week ago. And even closer to home than Noel, the eldest boy from the farm over the road hanged himself last week in one of the cowsheds.

><

29 February

I finished yet another draft of *Thin Woman* and sent it off to Jeremy Howe. Rose's Spanish journey reminds me more than ever of Robert Louis Stevenson's journey through the Cevennes with his donkey Modestine. Elk, her recalcitrant Morris Minor, acted as Rose's Modestine. Both travellers, Stevenson and Rose, experienced a terrible feeling of loneliness as they moved through the depopulated landscapes of France and Spain.

><

2 March

Funeral service for our neighbour's son at St Mary's. The church was packed out with young farmers looking awkward in suits, many of them weeping openly. We sang 'We Plough the Fields and Scatter', 'The Lord's my Shepherd' and 'Abide with Me' ('Change and decay/In all around I see ... Death, where is thy sting?/ And grave, thy victory?'). Long-haired Reverend Horseman did well with his fervent proclamations of the resurrection and the young man finding himself in a happier place. We came out into spitting grey rain and a biting wind.

9 March

Writing the first chapter feels like wading through mud. I have spent three days re-arranging it with no signs of improvement. Now back to the play again. The producer suggests the Merman tempt Rose with thoughts of suicide. Jeremy Howe considers the Merman too obvious a dramatic device and doesn't like him at all. And me? I'm beyond knowing.

16 March

Rugby Station is astonishingly dilapidated. It's not unlike Bristol Temple Meads in style, but in an advanced state of decay. What was it like in the Macaulays' day? Elegant probably, and doubtless served by more trains going to a wider variety of places. I sat in the Temple Reading Room of Rugby School and looked through the school lists and copies of *The Meteor* that Rusty Maclean had left out for me. Rusty Maclean! I would have liked to meet the owner of such a name, but alas, he was away at a conference somewhere. I didn't discover anything wondrous: George Campbell Macaulay taught at Rugby School for nine years, arriving a year before Parker Brooke, Rupert's father; he worked his way up the list of masters, teaching on the modern side when that was introduced by headmaster Jex-Blake in 1885. References to George Macaulay leaving, his obituary in the school magazine in 1915 etc, read as purely formal valedictions. There's actually no sign at all in the school magazine of his individual presence – no clubs, no societies – no feeling that he was popular with the boys. Perhaps he just kept himself apart ...?

Girls attend the school now: they wear full, sweeping skirts almost down to their ankles, and tweedy jackets like the boys, and look silly. In the afternoon some of the girls and boys came into the Reading Room and conversed in foppish, yet penetrating, upper-class voices.

At lunchtime, when the Reading Room closed, I ate a chilly sandwich in a chilly churchyard, bought a disposable camera – I'd forgotten to bring my own one – so that I could photograph the house where Rose was born, and warmed myself up with coffee in a smart coffee house. Then I took some photos of 11 Hillmorton Road, which Rusty Maclean had found out for me was where the Macaulays lived. Well, it's probably 11 – the Brooke house was number 3 then, but is 5 now, so the Macaulays might have lived in what's now number 9. But whether 9 or 11, it's one of two middle houses of a terrace of four; mid-Victorian, tall, elegant, with a rusting ironwork balcony on the first floor. I rang the bell, and the door was opened by a stammering Irish decorator, who directed me to a house round the corner where number 11's previous owner, a small, pleasantly plump woman, ushered me into a room chaotic with books, papers, and computer terminals on every available surface, and started digging around for old maps of the town. She had never heard of the Macaulays but kindly promised to find out all she could. She told me the row of four terraced houses was put up 'as a job lot' by a female entrepreneur between 1845 and 1860. While the men were busy expanding the empire, she said, the women were in rented houses in Rugby sending their boys to the school.

Must remember to check out the Married Women's Property Act. I'm reading Philip Pullman's *Tiger in the Well* and finding it almost unbearably painful. His heroine Sally Lockhart loses everything: money, stocks and shares, business, almost loses her small daughter, because a man who wants to ruin her claims that he is married to her. He simply goes into the bank and says that he is her husband: they hand over everything that is in her name.

17 March

I'm working on the Merman's story in *Thin Woman*, which ties in with the mermaid story in *And No Man's Wit*, the last novel Rose wrote before Gerald died. Jeremy Howe now thinks the Merman works OK. The play seems to have become a story about what Rose sacrificed for Gerald – family, friends, faith – everything except her writing, and now she can't write novels any longer. She has lost everything.

><

21 March

Spring Equinox. First Tuesday I haven't had to teach in six months.

><

22 March

I spent most of yesterday rewriting the first paragraph of the second chapter. It's ridiculous. This is only meant to be a first draft anyway – I need to be getting the stuff down, on paper, in just a rough order, rather than spending three hours moving one sentence from the end of the paragraph to the beginning and then back again.

><

29 March

I drove to Oxford yesterday. Like father, like daughters: the Macaulay girls didn't exactly shine out amongst their contemporaries at school in Oxford, nor did Rose later on at the university. At school Jean did just as well as Rose, judging from prizes and exam results. Rose went to Somerville in 1900. It was a non-denominational college, named for a scientist rather than a saint or church patron like the other women's colleges. Mary Somerville was a self-taught Scot who published her first book, *The Mechanism of the Heavens* aged fifty-one, and was the mother of six children. Apparently she was also 'a skilled needlewoman, a thrifty housewife, and a competent cook'.

In Somerville I pored over a booklet that contained water-colour illustrations, with accompanying texts, of the third years' going-down party in 1903, when those graduating were required to dress up as

2. Rose Macaulay as a Caterpillar in 'Privilege of Parliament' from the Somerville College 1903 Going-Down Play. By kind permission of the Principal and Fellows of Somerville College, Oxford.

their totem animal. Rose dressed up as a caterpillar. She was drawn nibbling leaves and grass, climbing and falling from twigs and stalks, and rowing a boat. The text proffers Rose as shy, absent-minded, mad keen on anything to do with ships (as she had been as a little girl) and ambitious – but with wings as yet undeveloped and therefore prone to failure. It suggests – behind the drollery of 'It has been known upon one occasion to consume a whole banana, but this can only be taken as an exceptional case, for the animal eat [sic] nothing during the twenty four hours preceding and following this phenomenal meal' – that she suffered from a chronic eating disorder. I think.

31 March

Anthony Powell died a couple of days ago. Various idiots have been on Radio 4 bleating about how he was shallow and snobby – and then boasting that they had never actually read the *Dance*, as if this were on their part an admirably high-minded refusal. In his contribution to 'The Pleasures of Knowing Rose Macaulay', which Constance reprinted in her biography, he wrote of a *Dance*-like exchange he and Rose had when they bumped into each other in Venice, a few months before she died:

'What on earth are you doing here?'

'I might well ask you the same question.'

'Oh, me?' she said, 'I'm just on my way to the Black Sea.'

4 April

Arctic winds, sleet and snow yesterday, TV transmitters down in Bristol and Bath. I met Pat Ferguson for a sandwich in Mud Dock. She told me her new novel is being considered by Black Swan. Pat continues to attend the writing group chez Geraldine Kaye that I used to be in, along with Diana Hendry and Viv French. She said that it now includes a militarily mustachioed man called Bruce, who at the last meeting advised Pat on the type of Spitfire she should be referencing in her story, and then read out an arresting retelling of Rumpelstiltskin, in which Rumpelstiltskin runs off with the queen and lives with her in a cosy ménage in the woods; poet Philip Lyons who ran the Creative Writing Diploma when Rowena Fowler was on sabbatical; and two women whose names Pat couldn't remember. Geraldine, as ever, presides. How she used to make Viv and me feel again like the sulky adolescents we once, long ago, both had been. Pat's mother is dying of cancer, her dog has a dislocated knee and is costing hundreds at the vet, and her nine-year-old son is too frightened to stay in his bed at night, and, when asked by his father to make a drawing of what was causing his anxiety (a suggestion from *How to Deal with an Anxious Child*, which Pat had bought), drew a picture of his mum and dad hanging dead by the neck next to a clown with huge claws brandishing a sword. Scary.

I hope Black Swan take Pat's novel. She is a good and subtle writer.

And now I must start the Oxford chapter.

6 April

I had written a note to Jonathan Hunt and he rang me in his lunch hour from a phone box outside the Fitzwilliam. I could hear the roar of traffic. He has visited Hillmorton Road in Rugby, and Tŷ-issa near Aberystwyth, where the Macaulays lived before Rose's father got the Cambridge job and they moved to Great Shelford, and which I visited last year with Michael Carson on our way to teach at Tŷ Newydd. I promised to send Jonathan a postcard from Varazze, to add to his Conybeare/Macaulay postcard collection. He told me George Macaulay had been turned down for jobs at Eton and Harrow. Aha. So perhaps when he landed one eventually at Rugby he thought it best just to keep his head down ...

I've had a painful back for the last two days and am hoping it won't get worse.

A chapter on Rose and Constance?

7 April

The trouble with doing research is that half the time you don't know what it is you're looking for, or at least what you might want to know, until after you've packed up your books and gone home. So, when I was in Somerville, looking at the booklet with the animal pictures of Rose and her contemporaries, the only name I recognised was that of her pal Marjorie Venables Taylor. Later, when I went to the High School, I discovered that Helen Darbishire (later Principal of Somerville) was a contemporary of Rose's at school, and that year won 'the Somerville exhibition'. So of course it would be nice to know how she appeared in 1903. Hurray for email – Pauline Adams has just replied to tell me that in the booklet Helen Darbishire was portrayed as a woolly grey sheep with a green handbag.

Kind, generous Jonathan Hunt has sent me a parcel of Conybeare material, which includes his transcript – not a copy, but his original – of the letter Eliza Conybeare wrote to her daughter Grace describing the final hours of her cousin Emilie Rose (for whom my Rose – Emilie Rose – was named); and he has written out for me the George Macaulay references in Francis Jenkinson's diaries.

✦

14 April

Schubert 'allows us to live with pain', says Claire Tomalin on *Desert Island Discs*. The consolations of music: you can feel the emotion and music contains it. Claire Tomalin was a glittering girl at Newnham, then fell into marriage and babies, with a philandering husband, who was killed (in Israel I think; he was a war correspondent) and so released her. But she had a baby who died at one month, then a baby born with spina bifida, and now, she's just said she had a brilliant beautiful daughter who died young. God! How could she bear it? She sounds extremely nice. On the subject of biography she said: say what it is you don't know. No-one ever wants to be written about, to be summed up. She is *fond*, she says, of all her subjects. Sue Lawley came across as envious of Claire Tomalin's achievements. 'Surely family is more important than your work?' she asked, in what sounded like an attempt to put her down. She would never say something like that to a man.

Am I fond of Rose? Yes. I think 'fond' describes it well. If you're fond of someone you don't have to unwaveringly like or admire them. You can feel exasperated at times. I feel exasperated by Rose when she's pedantic, or overly, disingenuously self-deprecatory. But she was a woman who struggled: for the life of the mind, for her art, for the life of the heart. She suffered considerably in that struggle, but she expressed herself in gaiety. She never lost – or only temporarily – the tomboyish girl child she once had been. Who wouldn't be fond of her?

✦

24 April

Dreamt last night that someone gave me a piece of music – manuscript or recorded? I can't quite remember – a mass or requiem, that Rose Macaulay had composed late in life. I had never even heard of it.

Chapter Four: April–May 2000

Italy/Devon/Home

Thursday 27 April

Arrived Genoa airport 1.15 pm local time having left home at 4.45 am. C and I have a room on the third floor of the Hotel Cairoli, in the old town, with church bells pealing outside the window, stone angels flying along the portico of the building opposite, and the stairwell covered in posters for animal and gay rights. Narrow paved or cobbled streets between majestic blocks of houses, where lines of washing loop between green-shuttered windows. Apparently a knife-thrust to the back was the most popular murder mode in these cramped narrow alleys, back in the days of the feuding Guelfs and Ghibbellines. We went into the small dark church of San Donato, then into a Jesuit church, Gesú, dripping with gilt and *trompe l'oeil* effects. Then the Cathedral of San Lorenzo, with Lorenzo on his griddle over the door, and some bizarre relics and reliquaries in the crypt, including a round chalcedony platter, on which Salome ('tis said) carried the head of St John the Baptist. Various saints' bones, and, displayed in a monstrance like a trapped spider, a lock of the Blessed Virgin's hair.

Friday 28 April

Cogoleto, the next bay north of Varazze. We're in the Hotel Miramar which does indeed overlook the sea. After a day of low pressure and intermittent rain, waves crash on the beach. The Italians are out in hats and umbrellas, and their babies muffled up as if it were mid-winter. I'm in cotton trousers and a T-shirt. We took the train west, and then south, from Genoa's Stazione Prinzipe (failed to validate our tickets in the machine, so the ticket woman – unarmed luckily, unlike all other uniformed people here – wrote on the backs, 'clienti stranieri', with a look on her face of profound sadness) past miles of rusting steel works, rusting engines on rusting weedy sidings, acres of grey containers and dark green derricks, with not a soul in sight, then through tunnel after tunnel, and then Cogoleto, nestled between steep hills (autostrada flying across the top) and the sea shore, a few streets of pink- and orange-washed houses with green shutters, some bars along the seafront.

We had bruschetti and panini outside a bar at lunchtime. The panini have different fillings depending on the month: April's is *tonno* and *pomodoro*. Then we took the train down to Varazze, where we found narrow Via San Ambrogio, and number 6, where the Macaulays first lived in 1887. Round the corner a funeral was in process in Piazza San Ambrogio, where the saint himself raises his scourge in a niche in the wall opposite the entrance to the church. Later all the old men stood around outside the church chatting, while the women went in and muttered their devotions in front of the statue of Santa Caterina. We walked in search of the *Villa Macolai*, the square red house by the sea, and walked, and walked ...

What did I hope to find here in Varazze? I hoped to catch a glimpse of the eight- or ten- or twelve-year-old Rose running barelegged down the beach and throwing herself into the boat and rowing out to sea, or to hear an echo of the children's shouts as they chased the goat that once again had slipped its tether, or as they surfed the waves that crashed into the basement rooms of the *Villa Macolai* during the autumn storms.

I think I hoped to be able to see back through the intervening century to find Varazze as it was a hundred years ago, to see it as Rose saw it and somehow to feel in myself what Rose felt. And I wanted perhaps to recapture the unfetteredness I myself felt as a little girl beneath the East African sun, by following Rose back to the place beneath the Italian sun where she felt most free. Those early novels of hers yearn for it.

Part of the biographical urge comes from wanting to experience the world as someone else experienced it, seeing it through someone else's eyes. Doesn't it? Wasn't that the desire that in 1964 drew Richard Holmes to the Cevennes in the footsteps of Robert Louis Stevenson and his donkey Modestine?

On the walls of the corridors in the Communale hang a series of blown-up photos of Varazze in the early 1900s, showing the limits of the town just beyond the chiesa de Santa Caterina, pretty much where I think the *Villa Macolai* was situated. Rose's published recollections

3. Varazze and a crowded sea, around 1900, from a contemporary
   postcard. Comune di Varraze.

of Varazze suggest it was a sleepy fishing village. The photographs on
the walls show a very grand Grand Hotel, bathing huts lined up along
the beach, and, in place of the empty sea of Rose's recollections, a
sea jampacked with people playing ball games and generally horsing
around and acting like holiday-makers.

Perhaps life with 'the Five' was so intense she didn't notice the
day trippers and holiday-makers; so self-sufficient that the presence
of strangers didn't impinge? Or did she need an old-fashioned and
underpopulated Varazze for the lost paradise of her imagination?

Sat 29 April

I've found no trace of the Macaulays' seven year residence here, except, solely, a record of Gertrude's death, aged three years and six months, in the register of deaths for 1892. Grace records, in one of the diaries that I read in the Wren, that the little bit of pocket money belonging to Gertrude when she died of meningitis was spent on lockets for the other children, which they were given on New Year's Day 1893 – each one presumably containing a lock of Gertrude's legendary golden hair. What an albatross for poor unloved Eleanor.

Rose brought Gerald O'Donovan here in the early days of their love affair and stayed – I think – in the village we're staying in, Cogoleto.

><

Sunday 30 April

Feast of Santa Caterina. At 10 o'clock we're in Piazza San Ambrogio for the start of the procession. Groups of men in white cotton smocks and short velvet capes – red, blue or black – enter the square carrying huge glittering crucifixes. The carriers wear a leather harness strapped over their shoulders and chest, with a thick leather pouch at the waist into which the pole of the crucifix is slotted. Each crucifix has its own group of about ten men, each of whom takes a turn with the burden. A massive black Christ on the cross is carried by the group of heftiest-looking men – middle-aged blokes in black capes. A group of younger slenderer men, in their early twenties perhaps, sporting red capes, stagger beneath a medium-sized crucifix which, according to a knowledgeable German tourist – the only other tourist in sight – weighs 100 kilos. Two smaller crucifixes are carried, respectively, by a group of teenage boys and by a group of old greybeards. Girl guides, scouts, little ones in long robes, mill around. At 11 o'clock the doors of San Ambrogio open and Santa Caterina is carried out standing on a bed of bobbing white marigolds, while four policemen in plumed hats take up a vanguard position with their swords pointing heavenwards. The procession moves off, and everyone bursts into song, and I hear the hymn just as Rose and her brothers and sisters must have heard it over a hundred years ago:

4. Contemporary photograph of the procession on the Feast of Santa Caterina, Varazze. Comune di Varraze.

Difendi, O Caterina,
Da peste, fame e guerra,
Il popolo d'Italia
In mare e in terra ...
Difendi, O Caterina,
Da guerra e terremoto
Il popol di Varazze
A te devoto!

(Save, O Caterina, From plague, and want, and war, The people of Italy, From the hilltops to the shore ... Save, O Caterina, From war and earthquake's roar, The people of Varazze, Who always you adore!)

This makes up for the lack of any trace of Rose, for the disappearance of the square red house by the sea, for the distance I've been feeling from her.

We nip ahead of the procession and station ourselves outside the Chiesa de Santa Caterina as everyone arrives. Crowds of people in their Sunday best, the little girls in brightly coloured frocks and white tights, and the little boys in neatly pressed khaki baggy shorts and loose T-shirts, babies in state-of-the-art buggies and cotton sun hats, many clutching the strings of helium-filled Pikachus, which float glittering in the air next to the glittering gold and silver of the painted flowers bedecking the crucifixes. The difference between now and then? People chatting on their mobiles as they cheer and clap the procession; the honking of horns, and engines revving from scooters and motorbikes and cars bringing up the rear.

><>

Wednesday 3 May

I have been re-reading Richard Holmes's *Footsteps*. Holmes was only eighteen when he set out through the Cevennes in the footsteps of Stevenson. Quite early on in the journey he has a moment of revelation: he hallucinates that Stevenson is waiting for him, that he'll meet him on the bridge over the river Allier, and then he looks downstream and sees the ruins of the old bridge, the one that Stevenson must have crossed. And he realises that the bridges are down, that he can't cross over into the past, that he won't, ever, meet Stevenson. That night he has a mad dream of children mocking him, dancing and singing on the broken bridge of Avignon, and interprets it as a warning: not to be so childish and literal-minded in his pursuit. But instead to accept the necessary gap, the historical distance, and use other skills and 'sensible magic' to make the unattainable past come to life again. The process of biography, he writes, 'was to become a kind of pursuit, a tracking of the physical trail of someone's path through the past, a following of footsteps. You would never catch them; no, you would never quite catch them. But maybe, if you were lucky, you might write about the pursuit of that fleeting figure in such a way as to bring it alive in the present' (Holmes 1985, 27).

><>

Wednesday 10 May

Devon coast, near Thurlstone Sands, where we're recording the sea sequences of *Thin Woman in a Morris Minor*. At the read-through yesterday afternoon it became obvious that my script was too long by about twenty minutes. I stayed up very late, until 2 am, making massive cuts – about a quarter the length of the play – and feeling bitterly upset with the producer for her failure to notice earlier that it was much too long for a forty-five minute slot.

But Maureen O'Brien is perfect as Rose Macaulay. She's able to be witty, clever, sad, self-mocking, lyrical, and all the things that I wanted the character to be. The actors all bravely splashed and swam in the cold sea, well beyond the call of duty, and lovely Ilsa the sound manager put on a wetsuit and did the swimming bits for Maureen as Maureen recited her lines. There was a strong feeling of camaraderie, and as Maureen spoke the words I felt that life was being breathed into them, and that Rose herself would not have disapproved.

19 May: Home

I'm embarking anxiously on my section on Rose and Rupert Brooke. Am I completely mad to think that perhaps Rupert stole the honey and the tea from Rose? I first started thinking this last year when I looked up the months of publication of *The Valley Captives* and 'The Old Vicarage, Grantchester' and found that *The Valley Captives* came out in January 1911, and 'The Old Vicarage' was published the following year, first as 'The Sentimental Exile' in the King's College magazine and then a few months later in the first volume of *Georgian Poetry*. In February 1911, the month after *The Valley Captives* came out, Rose and Rupert shared the two guinea poetry prize in the *Saturday Westminster*. He was a regular visitor to the Macaulays in Great Shelford. Surely it's inconceivable he didn't read her novel?

'Will there be honey for tea, please, Susan?' asks Tudor Vallon, desperately seeking escape in a remembered childhood sanctuary, but expecting the answer 'no'. 'And is there honey still for tea?' asks Brooke's sentimental exile a year later, expecting the answer 'yes'. Rose's novel is tragic; Rupert's poem satiric.

The inhabitants of Great and Little Shelford – the Shelfordians – provide one of the many targets for Brooke's satire. But are their 'twisted lips and twisted hearts' a payback for Rose's *Views and Vagabonds*, her satire of Brooke's Fabian-inspired romanticisation of the rural working-class, and in particular of the caravan trips he'd recently made through the southern English countryside trying to stir up the peasantry to a sense of their own oppression? *Views and Vagabonds* came out in February 1912, just a month or so before Rupert went off to Germany where he composed 'The Sentimental Exile'.

Or is this altogether too fanciful?

As I discovered in the British Library when I was comparing Rose's and Rupert's published poetry in the *Westminster Gazette*, plenty of women were published in its poetry pages by Naomi Royde-Smith. But no women were included by Edward Marsh – loving mentor of Brooke and architect of his posthumous fame – in the first three volumes of his 'Georgian' poetry anthologies, which drew heavily on the male *Westminster Gazette* poets. He wanted a female contributor for his fourth volume, and chose Fredegond Shove (daffodils, cows, sheep and Jesus) over the other three women suggested to him: Rose Macaulay, Charlotte Mew and Edith Sitwell. In the fifth and final volume two women appeared: Alice Meynell and Vita Sackville-West.

It was generous Naomi Royde-Smith who helped out after Brooke's breakdown (the first of his breakdowns?) in 1913 by getting him a commission to travel to America and write about it.

Chapter Five: June 2000

Cambridge/Home

June 4: Cambridge

On Sunday afternoon I met Jonathan Hunt. Because of his formal-sounding, precise way of talking, and his neat precise handwriting, I had imagined him as an elderly man, in his late sixties perhaps, but he's much younger than I'd thought. On Sunday I thought he was perhaps fifty, but later on in the week, because of references he made to my own time as an undergraduate, he seemed to be implying that he's younger than I am, perhaps forty-four or forty-five. His flat off the Chesterton Road was clean, sparse, barely – in a bare style – furnished. He showed me file after file of Conybeare material: photocopies of a photo album he'd found in – I think – Diana Lindsay's house. She was a McCormick – Alison's granddaughter? He also had material from Ruth Conybeare – daughter of Bruce, who, in their family legend, was made to feel a miserable failure by his father Edward. We ranged widely. I was able to tell him that Edward and Grace's father, Rose's grandfather, the Rev W J Conybeare, had been blinded in one eye when he was fourteen, after having a stone thrown in his face by a boy at school. Jonathan pressed on me two of his Conybeare notebooks, one of them a full transcript of a year of Edward's diary, the other with incredibly detailed Conybeare family trees. Did he want to publish? I asked. No. His work on Conybeare is an escape for him from AD 2000.

I was staying in Barton Road with my friend Tessa's mother Sheila, widow of J P (Peter) Stern the historian, in her handsome L-shaped house, built for the Sterns by architect friends when Peter got a fellowship at St John's in the 1950s. The garden leads down to the Barton Road secret lake. When Tessa was a child they had a rowing boat; now the remains of a wooden jetty rot quietly in the water. Staying with Sheila is ever so much more fun than being on my own in Newnham: she's a mistress of scurrilous university gossip, and mistress too of the dry martini. Why has nobody ever told me before of the wonders of dry martinis?

Monday

I started reading in the Wren. I love it: the silence, the hiddenness of it, the way a group of strangers sits around a table all day not speaking to each other, each one immersed in a separate world. I had meant to spend less than a day on those of Grace's diaries that I hadn't read last year; in the end I was reading them until Wednesday morning. At the beginning of the week the hours seemed to stretch out ahead as if without end – I was confident I would read all I wanted to. By Thursday I was reading faster and faster, desperate to get as much past my eyes in the shortest possible time as I could.

On Monday afternoon, after the library closed, I went to have high tea – fresh eggs from a friend's hens, tea, bread, hummus, cheese, fruit cake – just what I needed – with Philippa Pearce in King's Mill Lane in Great Shelford, in one of the millworkers' cottages, built by her grandfather, that she now lives in.

When I described Jonathan's eccentric solitariness to Philippa she said, 'Hmm, not the kind of person you would want to be alone with in his flat,' and I said, 'Well, yesterday I was, for four hours.' I told Philippa that I had felt momentarily anxious when I'd gone in, and that since then I'd been feeling guilt about that anxiety. He may be eccentric but he couldn't be more generous.

Philippa and I walked round the meadow, purple and yellow with clover and buttercups, with her black labrador, along the bank of the Cam, then to the Mill House where she grew up, a Georgian style mid-Victorian square brick house, now owned by a rich couple, and to the beautiful old mill itself, where her father was the last ever miller to mill there. When she was little her mother used to send her over to the mill to check that it was OK with the man in charge of the generator before she plugged in the iron to do the ironing. The new owners of the mill house weren't at home, so Philippa took me in to show me round the walled garden: her, or rather Tom's, Midnight Garden. I'd been reading Philippa's first book, *Minnow on the Say*, on Tessa's recommendation. As we watched the waters of the Cam rushing and leaping through the mill race under the King's Mill I could see the exact picture of the miller in *Minnow* leaning over the bridge at Folly Mill. Then we walked up the bank of the river towards the village recreation ground, which is on land once owned by the Macaulays; along the bank where once stood Rose's beloved boat house, a corner of which can be glimpsed in the photo that appears as the frontispiece to *The Secret River*. Grace had a hut on what is now the recreation ground, in which she used to instruct the village girls in Christianity and good behaviour, and where she sometimes used to sleep – until driven out by the fleas brought in, she complained, by Mr Pearce's – Philippa's grandfather's – hens. Philippa and I worried that it seemed an awfully long way for the hens to have travelled, all the way from the King's Mill up the riverbank to Southernwood.

Philippa was interested to hear of Jonathan Hunt's Conybeare researches. There were Pearce millers at Barrington, apparently, in the 1860s, so she hoped they might appear in uncle Edward C's diaries. When did he take up the Barrington living? 1870 something? I told her Jonathan had suggested we go out to Barrington. Maybe Philippa could come too? She remembered her father pointing out a house at the far end of the village green (the largest village green in England, 'tis said by someone or other) and saying his forebears had lived there.

On Tuesday after the Wren Library closed I went out to see Dr Barbara Reynolds on the Milton Road. Now aged 86, Barbara Reynolds is god-daughter and biographer of Dorothy L Sayers and editor of her letters. Carolyn Caughey at Hodder had put me in touch with her. Barbara dispensed tea and doughnuts from a trolley in her book-lined study, and we discussed the possibility that Aunt Dot in *The Towers of Trebizond* – plump, square-faced and with brilliant blue eyes – is modelled on Dorothy L Sayers. As evidence Barbara read out loud to me Aunt Dot's speech, at the end of the novel, about belief and grief. She pointed out that it not only accurately reproduces the rhythms of DLS's speech, but also the pragmatical nature of her religious belief. Rose and DLS were amongst those who used to hang out at St Anne's House in Soho in the 1950s, chattering in a highbrow way of faith and form and function. When Dorothy L Sayers died in 1957 Rose was one of the only four mourners present at the interment of her ashes at the foot of the St Anne's tower. (Present: Rose, Barbara Reynolds herself,

Fleming (son of DLS), Mrs Fleming, with Father Patrick McLaughlin officiating.)

On my return home I found a letter from the delightful Barbara elaborating further this hypothesis with reference to Aunt Dot's various church speeches throughout *The Towers of Trebizond*, and suggesting too that Father McLaughlin might have been the model for Father Chantry-Pigg. (Chantry: I often wonder if this is an Anthony Powell reference, Chantry being the name of the Somerset village where he lived. A little fanciful perhaps.) Critical/biographical interpretations of *Towers* tend to be so po-faced and pious; it seems to me not at all unlikely that Rose should take the opportunity in a novel about faith and religion to have fun at the expense of a priest she was acquainted with, and to tease her high Anglican friend Dorothy L Sayers.

Rose herself was not immune to the deadening effect of piety: see her *Last Letters* to Father Hamilton Johnson. But of course Hamilton Johnson, the recipient, was hardly a bundle of laughs, and as Mary Anne O'Donovan, Gerald O'Donovan's grand-daughter said to me on Thursday, those letters were private. Of course she's right. They weren't written with publication in mind. Had they been, they might have been wittier, more polished ...

Wednesday

Glancing again at Grace's 1879 commonplace book *Morning Light*, I noticed this time the cross on 18 February, marking a miscarriage eight weeks after her wedding. In her diary she writes 'taken ill'; she uses the same phrase to record her sister-in-law Frances Conybeare going into labour. Perhaps Frances was the first young woman Grace knew at all closely to give birth; very possibly Grace didn't know what it entailed.

In the morning I'd rung the owners of Southernwood to ask if I could go out again, after the library closed, and see round the inside of the house. Confusion on the phone as Mrs B, who's slightly deaf, thought, when I said my name, that I was someone wanting to speak to her daughter Sarah. Got that sorted out with her son's help, and I asked if I could come just for twenty minutes. In the event I was there for three hours, becoming increasingly anxious as I'd promised to take

Sheila Stern out for dinner, but Mr and Mrs B wanted to show me, very sweetly, but very slowly, every inch of the house, every tessellated corner, every line of picture rail. I would have liked to stand alone in an upstairs bedroom, or to walk down the wide wooden staircase past the stained glass birds and flowers at the bottom and to have looked out quietly into the garden and at the trees that Rose and Margaret used to climb. Rose wrote seven novels in this house. I left at nine o'clock. By then Sheila had made a salad for us and taken some smoked salmon out of the deep freeze. We had two dry martinis each to revive us. Oh wonderful Sheila.

Sheila told me the story of how Peter had been turned down for the Chair at Cambridge because he was deemed 'too intellectual', and so went to University College London instead, where his intellectualism was appreciated. So who did get the Cambridge Chair? I asked. A fellow who'd written one fusty musty volume on the use of one particular German word in 13th century monastic manuscripts, said Sheila with scorn.

Meanwhile I'd struck up a friendship in the Wren with another reader, the only other one who'd been there, like me, every day since Monday: a guy called Patrick who's working on a biography of Rab Butler. Every so often we would encounter each other outside the gates of New Court and have hurried conversations, commiserating with each other on the amount of time it takes to read, and how do you know what to take notes on before you've read enough to know what's going to turn out to be significant? I've been taking too many notes, I suspect. And it really slows down the reading. Patrick takes notes on a laptop, which he says he got cheaply second-hand. It would really save time not to have to type up notes when I get home.

With a joyful start of recognition I read in one of Rose's letters about the *Fabled Shore* trip, writing of the warning she'd received from the consul's wife in (I think) Madrid: 'Not a single one of Mrs Mortimer's bandits has crossed our path and I feel almost disappointed'. I have already given Rose a bold carelessness about bandits in *Thin Woman in a Morris Minor*, and to have had confirmed what I had only imagined feels like a good omen.

On Tuesday I had a terrible fright. In the Wren it's normally quiet as the grave, with just the dry rustle of ancient pages being turned, interrupted only when the front-desk librarian rings through to the scholars' table to arrange a shift change with whoever's on duty, or to report on the status of an ordered item. The supervisor picks up and answers quietly; it barely disturbs us readers. On Tuesday afternoon the supervisor answered the phone and then, his voice polite but with eyebrows raised, said, 'It's for you, Sarah.' My heart nearly stopped. Who would dare ring for a reader in the Wren? It could only be a dire emergency at home. And then within seconds I guessed. Emergency or no, only one person would dare ring a reader in the Wren, only one person would get through to the Wren: Sheila Stern. Sure enough, it was Sheila offering to come and pick me up because there was a thunderstorm (which I hadn't even realised), and it would be easy for her because she had a special dispensation – but of course – to bring her car into Trinity New Court.

On Thursday a Japanese man sat opposite me and sniffed annoyingly every thirty seconds for an hour and a half. After he'd left the supervisor who came on duty found a book missing. Minor panic ensued and flustered phone calls to the entrance desk and to downstairs. Patrick and I gazed at each other with a wild surmise, transfixed by the thought of a stolen manuscript. Then it was traced to the photocopying room.

I left the library early on Thursday as Mary Anne O'Donovan, granddaughter of Gerald, and god-daughter of Rose Macaulay, had said I could go and see her, but it would have to be at 3.30 rather than after the library had closed. She lives in a newish house in a little close off the Cherry Hinton Road with a ragged front garden and a consulting room – she's a Jungian analyst – built on round the back. She's tall and plump with long greyish hair and a pleasant round face. About ten years older than me, I guess.

She received me coolly, and said she didn't have much time.

Why should she be anything other than cool? Why would she welcome a complete stranger coming to ask prying questions about her family, digging up private relationships and making them public in a book? By what right does a biographer reveal other people's secrets? I'd read Mary Anne's frigidly polite letters to Constance when Constance was working on her biography in the early 1960s. Constance was the soul of discretion on the subject of Rose and Gerald.

5. Sketch of Marjoric Grant Cook. By kind permission of Dr Mary Anne O'Donovan.

But Mary Anne thawed out over a children-doing-A-levels conversation, and then she said something about her mother and father, and I realised, having assumed they were dead, that in fact both were alive. (Must learn to question my assumptions more closely: assume all subjects are alive unless you know for certain otherwise.) Her father Dermod, said Mary Anne, hated talking about the past, and would get very upset if I tried to speak to him. I assured her I wouldn't.

No wonder she was distrustful of me, fearing I might go and upset her aged father.

When we started talking about Rose's work, Mary Anne became much friendlier. Her Rose is the clever, witty, accomplished Rose, not the tiresomely theological one. And her dislike of Constance, I realized, is related to Constance's churchy relationship with Rose – the fact that they met through the church and became friends during Rose's final churchy years – rather than the fact that she wrote a biography and was interested in the Rose/Gerald affair. 'We always felt Constance wormed her way in ...,' said Mary Anne. And published the Hamilton Johnson correspondence out of a desire to win fame for herself. Then her voice softened and she said, 'Well, that's what the family thought, that was the rumour.'

We went on to talk about Rose's friend, and godmother to Mary Anne's sister Jane, Marjorie Grant Cook, who, Mary Anne said, nursed Gerald in his last illness. Was she a nurse by training? I asked. 'No – but perhaps she did have some experience because she wrote a novel about a VAD in London in World War One who has an affair with a married man and then an abortion.' She stopped. 'Oh my god,' she said, and laughed. 'I hope the man wasn't based on Gerald. I'd never thought about that before.'

Must find out more about Marjorie Grant Cook – and read that novel!

><>

Later I dropped in at the nursing home to see Constance, and there met her niece-by-marriage (ex-marriage) Pat Babington Smith. I thought Constance was more alert than when I'd last seen her; she nodded her head as I talked to her, and held the flower card I'd written for her in her lap. Now and again she seemed to voice something, but no word that I could understand. God what a grim place. Pat says

6. Constance Babington Smith at work during the Second World War,
   studying an air reconnaissance photograph for evidence of the V1
   rocket. *Times*, 11 August 2000.

she thinks Constance is at peace. But how can she tell? She insisted I
borrow a copy of Constance's biography of some Russian woman who
had mystic experiences and then came to England and became Lady
somebody or other. Later, in the pub – I thought I'd better have a ham
sandwich before going out to Barrington with Jonathan Hunt, which
was just as well as I would have fainted with hunger otherwise – Pat
and I talked about older women and mother figures, like this

Russian woman was to Constance, and perhaps Rose was to her too. Constance's father, Henry, died when the children – a lot of them, nine or ten, I can't remember – were very young, and as Constance grew up she began to feel increasingly out of sympathy with her mother, who wanted her to be a young lady at home. Not unlike Rose's growing up, with father absent in spirit if present in flesh. Instead Constance dashed off and had adventures, and became an aerial photograph analyst and later made a major contribution to the war effort with her work on the German aircraft industry and her identification of the V1 at Peenemünde. And, like Rose, Constance too had a passionate love, but she lost him. Pat told me that when she, Pat, moved to Cambridge twenty years ago, adrift and with her family in tatters, Constance had been incredibly kind to her and helped her step back into the mainstream of life.

Then I went to Barrington with Jonathan Hunt, going via King's Mill Lane, where we discussed millers and non-conformists with Philippa Pearce. Philippa had told me beforehand that she was expecting a friend from the north who'd been at Girton with her in the 1920s (1930s, surely?). The friend turned out to be a wonderfully beady-eyed old bird whose grandfather had also been a miller – and non-conformist of course – in Croydon.

In the long-naved church at Barrington, the Church of All Saints, one of the stained glass windows is dedicated by Edward and Frances Conybeare's children, 'in gratitude for our happy childhood years in the vicarage'. Jonathan and I stood at the vicarage gate (I didn't feel quite up to going and banging on the door with Jonathan in tow) and I imagined George Macaulay and his brother and the other young undergraduate men – characterized by Edward as prowling lions and tigers – bicycling down the drive in their plus fours and tweed jackets to visit pretty, lively eighteen-year-old Grace when she was staying with her bearded patriarchal brother. Edward was vicar of All Saints for nearly thirty years. Then, poor fellow, the siren call of Rome became too insistent for him, so he had to give it all up. By our feet pale willow fronds trailed in the milky green Cam.

><>

June 12

Thin Woman in a Morris Minor was pick of the day in the Saturday *Telegraph* preview listings, the *Observer*, *Sunday Times*, *Mail on Sunday* and *Radio Times*. I couldn't stop grinning to myself all day. Gabriele Annan told me last week that she and Noel chose Spain for their honeymoon (1949? 1950?) because they'd just read *Fabled Shore*. Rose, said Gabriele, looked like 'a typical English schoolmarm', sitting on a sofa with her long thin legs tucked to one side. She was extraordinarily kind, and furnished them with introductions to all sorts of people in Spain and in Cyprus, including Lawrence Durrell (which surprised Gabriele, as she thought Rose much too nice a person to be a friend of Durrell's), and a Syrian called Mr McGubgub, who, when they met him, declared loudly: 'I am McGubgub of the McGubgubs'. This made me think of Mr Yorum in *The Towers of Trebizond* who bows to Laurie and says 'Yorum, Yorum, Yorum' in response to Laurie's 'who are you, sir?' when he appears in the foyer of the Yessilyurt Hotel as a consequence of Laurie misreading her Turkish phrase book and, believing that she's saying to the receptionist 'I do not understand Turkish', is in fact saying 'Please to phone at once to Mr Yorum' (Macaulay 1956, 156). Rose was always excellent witty and charming company, said Gabriele.

13 June

I just went over to the Farm to take them an advertising card for the broadcast later this week of *Thin Woman*, but when I knocked at the door Jack dashed out white-faced and visibly shaking all over: Uncle Martin's had a terrible accident. Is there anything I can do? I asked. – No, no, best just go, he said. I turned to see an old VW van – which I recognized as the doctor's van – rattling up the drive. I fear the worst.

14 June

The worst happened. Martin has killed himself. In the same way, and in the same place, as his son did only a few months ago.

16 June

Thin Woman was broadcast yesterday, sounding weirdly unlike what I had written. Various people rang or emailed later and praised it: Jill Nicholls, Diana Hendry, Mum and Dad, Pat Ferguson, Michael Carson, Stephen Hayward, Pippa Gladhill. Nikki Skinner, whom I hadn't heard from in five or six years, heard it in her car and stopped by the roadside to ring me up. In the *Guardian* Gillian Reynolds called it 'intriguing', and Peter Barnard in the *Times* called it 'a delightful evocation of both the physical territory and the emotional landscape.' Lovely people!

Part of the pleasure of writing drama is hearing (or seeing) what you've written animated by a different creative intelligence from your own, hearing it transformed as the actors act and the director directs. At moments I felt a joyful surprise. And at moments a dread puzzlement.

28 June

I've written chapters 4 and 5 very rough; too much, probably, about Rupert Brooke; I must consider what I've written and re-write it, but first I think I'd like to get up to – 'get up to'! – the beginning of the First World War, ie 1910-1914, *Views and Vagabonds*, *The Lee Shore* and *The Making of a Bigot*. Cornwall teaching has been cancelled next week; bad as regards money, but it means I can knuckle down and work on the next chapter every day, after this bitty, unproductive week.

Mon came for a visit on Sunday after a weekend in Hay-on-Wye, where she'd hunted out in the second-hand bookshops copies of *A Casual Commentary*, *Letters to a Sister* and *Letters to a Friend*, this last interleaved with some yellowing newspaper clippings, one of which is of an article by Harold Nicolson, from what he calls his pagan point of view, about Rose's religious faith; he defends Constance's publication of the letters and claims that Rose and Father Hamilton Johnson were fine correspondents.

Meanwhile Barbara Reynolds is more than ever convinced that Aunt Dot is an inspired and witty portrait of Dorothy L Sayers, and she's now putting forward two candidates as models for Father Chantry-Pigg. She wants us to write a paper and broadcast a dialogue on the subject.

Going Abroad arrived from Warwickshire County Library.

Just received a postcard from Mary Anne O'Donovan, saying she had enjoyed *Thin Woman*, as had her mother, and that her mother, who was a good friend of Rose's, would be very happy to talk to me. That's fantastic – especially considering that I didn't even know, before I met Mary Anne, that her mother was still alive.

Use the structural time-scale of *Told by an Idiot* as a structure for section one? And that of *Dangerous Ages*, or perhaps of *Keeping up Appearances*, as a structure for the 1920s chapter?

Chapter Six: July–December 2000

Home/London/Wales/Home/London/Home

4 July: Home

Almost daily letters from Barbara Reynolds on the possible identities of Aunt Dot and of Father Chantry-Pigg, culminating in a short piece, '*un ballon d'essai*' she calls it. 'Should I send it to the *Times Literary Supplement*, or to *Church Times*?' she writes.

'Why not both?' I reply.

6 July

May Sinclair's *The Divine Fire* (1904) has arrived via inter-library loan from the Regional Joint Fiction Reserve in Yorkshire. It was last in a lending library in Cardiganshire, on 26 Jan 1951 and still has the library inserts: a fine of one penny for the first overdue week, twopence each week thereafter. And Extracts from the Rules: 'If an infectious disease occurs in any house containing books from the Library, these will be handed to the Medical Officer of Health. Persons residing there will not use the Library until the house is declared free from infection.' As if libraries, then, were a part of a network of community services, and of community rules and regulations; places from which you were excluded if you posed a threat to the health and wellbeing of the community they served.

12 July

Catchwords and Claptrap, no. 4 in the Hogarth Essays, Second Series, arrived from Queen's University, Belfast, acquired by them 30 November 1926 and with two borrowings recorded on the faded slip: May 1945 and November 1958. Has it not been taken out since then? I wonder.

From the Authors' Foundation on Saturday, a cheque for £1550, the exact amount I had applied for, to go towards the Varazze trip, Cambridge visits, Trebizond ... I feel wonderfully validated: some people, I mean the judges – Orlando Figes, Shena Mackay, Douglas Matthews, Jilly Paver and Jo Shapcott – think the book I'm writing sounds interesting and worth supporting.

Back to the first chapter, to lick it, lick it, lick it into shape.

><

30 July

Only two writing days last week because I went up to London to see Mum and Dad and to record my piece about the internet for Radio 4's *Off the Page*. Christopher Bigsby presented. I liked him – he was unpushy and responsive and free of the stab-you-in-the-back egotism that most presenters display (although not me, I sincerely hope, when I was presenting *A Good Read*). The other guests were clever Sue Blackmore whose green and blue and red spiky hair had been dyed, she told me, by her 18-year-old daughter; and Simon Ings, who, Lisa Tuttle told me on the phone the day before, had once written such a vicious review of one of her books – for *Foundation* – that the typesetter had refused to set it. She (Lisa) thought she must have done something awful to him to have merited such a review, but all she could remember was once mildly criticising one of his stories in a writers' workshop.

I have been reading Barbara Reynolds' affectionate and sensitive biography of Dorothy L Sayers. I hadn't realised that Harriet Vane's experience with the 'free love' lover in *Strong Poison* was modelled on DLS's own affair with the American writer John Cournos. Poor Dorothy, so innocent and enthusiastic. What a disaster it all was. In 1920 DLS lived in number 36 St George's Square, Pimlico. I've written off to Michèle to ask if she remembers the number of the house that contained the flat that, in the summer of 1972, she and I shared with my brother Mark, Frances Wood, and a frightening Australian woman who tried to persuade Michèle and me to get our tubes tied. Thinking about the young Dorothy makes me nostalgic for my own London youth – eating sausages with Michèle on the balcony overlooking the square and listening to her tales of love and adventure among the stacks in the Printed Books Department at the British Museum, where she was a trainee librarian. Lord Peter Wimsey's Miss Climpson has a top-storey flat in St George's Square; I can't remember if the 'cattery' – Miss C's roomful of female sleuths disguised as a typing pool – was also housed in the square?

6 August

I haven't done much work this week, apart from a little reading of Gretton, whose understated wit I'm enjoying, but I'm only up to 1895. I get so anxious about not being able to work properly during school holidays.

Thinking further about the local suicides, I was reflecting on the conversation I recently had with Tessa during the course of which she told me that her mother-in-law had killed herself. Her aunt, J P Stern's sister (and I already knew this because Sheila Stern had told me) had killed herself too, twenty years after surviving the Nazi death camps. Tessa was wondering whether these things run in families, and suggesting that maybe one shouldn't acquaint one's children too closely with details of earlier family suicides. I was idly thinking that possibly every family has their own secret suicides, maybe it's all much more common than we think; and then suddenly it hit me that in fact we ourselves have two close family members who killed themselves: my mother's sister, and my mother-in-law's brother. Well, perhaps died in mysterious circumstances would describe their deaths more accurately. And yet up until now I have always thought that suicide is what happens to other families; we have no dark secrets, oh no, not us. And what about Will's Pete? There was nothing mysterious about that: it was a straightforward hosepipe from the exhaust into the car; yet none of our children know about it. They think he died suddenly, vanishing in the way that adults sometimes do. It is as if there's something contaminating, or corrupting, about suicide, some infectious darkness from which we must protect our children.

Part at least of what attracts me to Rose is her secretiveness.

And Dorothy L Sayers: she kept the biggest secret of all, surely. A child. When she visited her son at his foster mother's, she had to pretend to be his godmother. She couldn't confide in her parents, whom she adored, nor the man she loved, as he had abandoned her, nor the father of the baby, as he too had buggered off.

9 August

Pat Babington Smith rang last night to tell me that Constance died a week ago last Monday, swiftly, after a pneumonia.

><>

16 August

A couple of days ago Sara Davies came round with her little one and the little one's little friend. (The last time the little one was here he climbed into the back of her mini and lay down on the back seat. – What are you doing, Josh? – I'm playing that I'm dead.) She told me she was about to become incredibly busy because she's got six commissioned dramas to produce. How lovely, I say, grinding my teeth silently and thinking, why doesn't she submit one of my proposals for a commission? And terribly busy with a new poetry series ... to be presented by Peggy Reynolds. How lovely, I say again, teeth nearly ground down to the jawbone.

I feel desperate to write another play while what I learned from writing *Thin Woman* is still fresh in my mind – and to experiment with a different structure from the journey narrative.

On Tuesday I went to Grosvenor Chapel in South Audley Street and sat in the back pew on the left where Rose used to sit in the 1950s: a good but distant view of the altar, and an easy escape route. I've just remembered that Rose's mother Grace used to sit in the back pew on the left in St Mary the Virgin in Great Shelford in the 1910s – keeping an eye out for giggling amongst the village girls, and with a good view too of Aulay's (hideous and inappropriate) memorial in the side chapel. Grosvenor Chapel is nicely plain and light-filled, only five or ten minutes from the Serpentine, and five or ten from Hinde House. Both the Serpentine and the Chapel offered her a kind of shining peace, Rose said. Definitely something a bit pagan about Rose's Anglicanism. I went to Hinde House: art deco ironwork doors, a blue plaque: Rose Macaulay, writer, lived and died here. (Am I right in thinking A N Wilson was instrumental in getting the plaque put up?)

This is one of the reasons I like Rose: she lived a life which a part of me envies. No. She lived a life part of which I envy. Especially the flat in central London, that part.

I spent the rest of the afternoon in the British Library.

><>

12 September

Tŷ Newydd, Llanystumdwy: I managed to fill my tank despite the petrol shortage and drove here yesterday via Hodnet, home of Rose's paternal grandfather Samuel Herrick Macaulay. The old rectory, where the Macaulays lived, has been recently bought by people who must be millionaires: indoor staff *and* outdoor staff. At St Luke's church I saw the tombstone of Samuel Herrick Macaulay and his wife Anne Georgiana. They also have a plaque in the outside of the church wall, below which is set another plaque, in memory of their son Harry, Rose's black sheep uncle, who died in Siam when Rose was a girl in Varazze, and was never mentioned again in the Macaulay household.

A wonderful week at Tŷ Newydd having endless chats with Michèle, who drank large amounts of wine every night and was fearfully indiscreet but totally adorable. The students – apart from the obligatory mad woman – were all serious about writing and on top of that some of them were good at it, too. Paul Bailey was the guest reader and we were all terribly worshipful of him. I knew that it was through his good offices that Tŷ Newydd had got the money to pay the tutors the same fee that Arvon pays; what I didn't realise until Sally Baker told me on the last morning is that through Paul Bailey she has got a grant of close on £100,000 to ensure full disabled access to all the courses. She'd spent months and months on what they call 'bid-making' for the Lottery, only to have the bid rejected; Paul Bailey had written a letter and made a phone call. No wonder we were all so worshipful.

Home. I've just finished teaching a four-day intensive creative writing course for the University of Bristol's Access Unit, for people who are blind or visually impaired. It went well, although marred by one of the students being left behind by mistake when we all went out to the theatre. Fortunately her – entirely reasonable – rage and distress, which hardly abated over the next two days, seemed not really to affect the other members of the group. Julia was there for the second time: she lost her sight at the age of ten, and still – fifty years later – she won't admit it to others, won't use a cane, or braille. So she hasn't read a book since she was ten, goes to a writing group but can't do the exercises because she can't see to write, can't read her work back (to my annoyance) in my classes, yet writes with wonderful comic flair about her childhood and her mother. She recited to me a poem she'd written about her two daughters, who are horrible to her, and burst into tears at the end of it. It was a doggerel poem of heartfelt passion and grief. 'That's ... that's ... Shakespearian,' I said, feeling useless as I patted her on the arm. She lives with a man – 'oh, Jim's such a kind man, a real gentleman' – who doesn't speak to her for days on end and expects her to keep the place spick and span. When he wants something he points at it rather than asks for it. 'He hates it when I talk in the car – but of course I understand that, Sarah, he doesn't want to be distracted ... but you know when we go out to a restaurant he won't say a word to me. He's very very shy ... If I didn't go out to my evening classes, weeks would pass without anyone speaking to me.' I want to go round and give him a great big kick up the backside, the nasty sadist. And a kick to her ungrateful daughters too.

28 September

Just remembered Mark Farrell telling a story of how he'd been talking at length to the Admissions Tutor at the college his eldest girl is going to. 'Yes, Dr Garcia, no Dr Garcia' etc. When he came off the phone, Olivia asked: Why did you keep on calling him Dr Garcia?
    Mark: That's his name, isn't it?
    Olivia: No, (you fool)! It's Dr Goss.
    Mark had heard his 'Dr Goss here' on answering the phone as 'Dr Garcia'. It made me laugh.

2 October

Where did I read Rose's 'The Empty Berth'? I know I've read it, but I can't find any notes on it, nor any reference to what anthology it might be in. It was published in the *Cornhill Magazine* in 1913. Or haven't I read it? Do I just think I have? Oh God, and my head is crammed full to bursting with all the stuff I have to teach this term, starting tomorrow:

Woolf, Sayers, Lehmann … and a day school on Barbara Pym. Why oh why did I say yes to the day school? Answer: Because it's paid work.

✺

3 October

Found 'The Empty Berth' in the *Cornhill Magazine* in the library. I hadn't read it, I realised as soon as I did read it, but had only read about it. It is utterly delightful, with a Forsterian lightness and grace in its portrayal of nuances of social class and the narrowness of the middle-class English soul.

Various thoughts have been flitting through my mind about a radio drama based on the story of Dorothy L Sayers and the baby she gave away; the men who let her down; and her creation of Lord Peter Wimsey.

✺

6 October

I emailed Mary Anne O'Donovan yesterday asking *inter alia* about the 'O'Donovan papers' which are referenced by both John Ryan, who wrote his PhD on Gerald, and Jane Emery, Rose's second biographer after Constance. Her reply: 'What are the O'Donovan papers? Should I know? Are they just the odd bits of things lying around in a suitcase in the attic?' I do rather like Mary Anne. And she has given me Muriel, her mother's, telephone number.

✺

11 October

I can't do any work on Rose with only two days to go to the Barbara Pym day school. I have lost my earlier enthusiasm for Pym. I hate the way her characters 'chortle', and the way they say things 'hopefully', 'timidly', 'rather nervously'. I want to get them by the scruffs of their necks and shake them until all their annoying adverbs drop away.

✺

17 November: London

Wednesday morning I took the Central Line from St Paul's – having spent the night in Michèle's apple-green studio, and had croissants with her for breakfast – to Holland Park, where Muriel Thomas, daughter-in-law of Gerald O'Donovan, mother of Mary Anne and Jane, and good friend of Rose's – lives in a basement flat, which she acquired through wartime Hungarian contacts. The rest of the house, a big handsome Regency building, has been bought by a barrister who's now trying to winkle her out.

Muriel reminisced wonderfully about holidays at the end of the 1940s in Italy and Spain with Dermod (her ex-husband, Gerald's son) and Rose. She remembered them all swimming at Varazze, but didn't remember seeing the square red house, the *Villa Macolai*, so perhaps it had gone by then. It all sounded such fun with Rose – who was high-handed, intrepid, and, surprisingly, useless at foreign languages. Then she went on to talk about the O'Donovans, whom, she told me, she did not like one little bit, not even her husband Dermod who she said bullied her into marrying him in Bombay during the war. She said his 'awful' mother Beryl was beastly to her overweight and sweet-natured youngest daughter Mary. Beryl told Muriel, soon after meeting her, that Dermod had had an illegitimate child by a 'Nurse Roberts' who'd turned up on the doorstep with babe in arms and had been sent away 'without a penny'. Muriel was told never to mention it. Gerald was old and ill by the time Muriel met him. I guess she would probably have been immune to his charm anyway, seeming to have taken against O'Donovans in general.

But he must have been charming, to have won and kept the love of Rose and of Marjorie Grant Cook for so many years.

Muriel poured two large glasses of sherry at lunchtime, and we shared a quiche. How wonderful for Rose to have found a friend like her where presumably she was not expecting it. It was Rose who was despatched by the O'Donovan family to meet Muriel when she returned, alone, but as Dermod's new wife, to England from Bombay, disembarking in Southampton one dark winter's night.

When I got home I rang William, the academic to whom I'd sent a copy of my original proposal for the biography, and who I hoped would write a reference for me for a British Academy small research grant to send me to the Harry Ransom Research Centre in Austin, Texas to look at the correspondence they hold there. He barely said hello, but launched into: 'There's no point in you applying to the British Academy. Your book simply isn't scholarly and adds nothing to the sum of human knowledge.' Well, fuck you, I did not say, but thought. He then informed me that his own proposal for a book on some minor Victorian novelist (my words not his) had recently been turned down; and of course his book would be both original and scholarly. I was shaken, upset, close to tears.

1 December

Terrible frustration with my chapter on the Great War. It creaks and plods and I don't really know what I'm saying about Rose and the war; I've been stuck on it all autumn. Reading the descriptive section on the war in *Told by an Idiot* I found myself getting annoyed with Rose for not being sharp like Virginia Woolf was sharp, for muddling and muddying it, for sitting on the fence, for saying: the war meant this for this person, that for that person. I found myself for the first time feeling actively hostile towards her.

I suspect I'm blaming Rose for my inability to get on with writing this chapter. I desperately need a clear space with no teaching. I'm doing a day school on women poets the weekend after this, and haven't even begun to think about it. And then there's all next term's reading still to do. Meanwhile a librarian at the Harry Ransom Research Centre will send me a copy of the Rose Macaulay card catalogue, and Muriel Thomas has unearthed six 'chatty' letters from Rose that she 'can't recollect proffering' to Jane Emery, which she's going to photocopy and send.

13 December

Spent yesterday in the Central Library reading Marjorie Grant Cook's *Latchkey Ladies* (published 1921 under the name M. Grant) – sent over from Trinity College Dublin and not allowed out of the library – which passionately explores marriage versus the single life, and, if I'm not mistaken, gives us an affair between Marjorie and Gerald O'Donovan. So perhaps Mary Anne's flash of insight was right? In the novel the O'Donovan figure's wife is called Rose: Rose! Anne Carey, with whom he is having an affair, gets pregnant and has a baby. My God! If MGC had an affair with Gerald, then what was the Marjorie/Rose relationship when Rose and Gerald started *their* affair? In 1921 Rose published *Dangerous Ages*. Her own novel about illegitimate babies – *What Not* – had already come out in 1919.

In 1949 when Rose visited Loughrea to see where Gerald had been a parish priest fifty years earlier, she was accompanied by her old friend Marjorie. If Marjorie had been his lover, too …

Chapter Seven: January–June 2001

Home/Cambridge/Home/London

20 January: Home

Chimney fire on Twelfth Night. House full of smoke and a roaring in the chimney like an aeroplane trying to get out. Firemen arrived with an iron bucket, a stirrup pump and a small driver's mirror that they must have rescued from a scrap merchant, which they hoped would help them see round the bends in the chimney. Poking rods up the chimney made no difference, so they got out the ladders and climbed on the roof and poured water down. 'Give him more of a drink,' they shouted from below. A shiny brown liquid began to ooze out from behind the picture rail in the sitting-room. The fire chief, whom I recognised as our part-time postman and part-time butcher's assistant, said admiringly, 'I haven't seen walls ooze like that for thirty years.' For days afterwards there was a disgusting smell of wet ashes; the towels all stank because the airing cupboard was full of smoke but I couldn't wash them because the washing machine was broken. Meanwhile I've started teaching but I don't want to be reading Chopin and Cather and McCullers because I want to be getting on with Macaulay.

><>

25 January

Spent the day in Cambridge yesterday in Mary Anne O'Donovan's house, looking at what Jane Emery and John Ryan refer to as the 'O'Donovan papers', but which could be called the Louisa Williams papers, as the vast bulk of them are letters between Beryl O'Donovan, née Verschoyle, and her grandmother in Rome, Louisa Williams. I read Beryl's typescript memoir, *Locust Food*, no mention of Rose, nor Marjorie, no mention of Rose anywhere, but then I found a letter from Rose to Beryl in 1941 condoling over the horrid death of Mary, Beryl and Gerald's youngest child, saying what a lovely girl she had been; later a postcard from Rose to Beryl from University College Hospital in 1950 something, saying no don't come and visit me as I'm coming out soon. So there was some kind of relationship between the two women. The letters were crammed higgledy-piggledy in a huge trunk which Mary Anne had dragged down from the attic. Then she flung open a drawer in a desk downstairs in the sitting room and invited me to have a look through a pile of letters she'd taken from her aunt Brigid's flat after Brigid's death, many of which were from Dermod (Mary Anne's father, Brigid's brother) to his father Gerald, 1930s from Poland and Spain, 'darling Daddy', 'dearest Daddy' etc. Me to Mary Anne: 'These are intimate and chatty, aren't they?' Mary Anne: 'D'you mean effusive? Creepy, I'd say.' It was an odd sensation sitting in her house looking at all this stuff to do with her father. She said two or three times, as she handed me a cup of coffee, or put her head round the door, 'we're a family who never spoke much.' And she told me the story of Dermod's illegitimate child, and its mother turned away by Beryl and Gerald, just as Muriel had told me. 'I just can't understand them at all,' said Mary Anne, meaning her father and grandfather, Dermod and Gerald. But she liked Beryl her grandmother, and affectionate dotty Gladys her great-aunt. Whereas Muriel preferred Gerald to Beryl, and made him Mary Anne's godfather.

Stuffed into a plastic bag I found a number of letters to Gerald dated 1910: well done for leaving the priesthood, congratulations on your marriage; and 1913: mainly in praise of *Father Ralph*, with one angry correspondent accusing him of heresy. John Betjeman wrote a few years later: he and his wife were going to Ireland and he was worried that his wife might be tempted over to Rome so he wanted her to read *Father Ralph* so as to be properly put off, and where could he get hold of a copy? (If he did get one it obviously didn't have the desired effect on Mrs B.)

Mary Anne's consulting rooms are in a detached brick building out the back of her house. Full of spiders, she said. Me, jokily: 'That sounds appropriately symbolic – of all sorts of things.' Mary Anne, darkly: 'Destructive mothers, you mean.' She certainly doesn't seem a destructive mother herself. Her own sturdy cheerful 18-year-old daughter was munching cheese on toast in the kitchen at lunchtime before going off to waitress at Starbucks.

29 January

I've just realised that all Mary Anne's comments on 'my family were very good at not talking ... my family are brilliant at not discussing things ...' etc are expressions of a recent hurt. Muriel said to me when I met her: 'When Boo (Mary Anne) turned up *the other day* and said, "I've got a half sister, haven't I?", I told her about Dermod and Nurse Roberts ...' I have only just remembered that phrase: *the other day*. Which suggests that Mary Anne has only recently found out about the existence of a half-sister; or has only recently had it confirmed by her mother. No wonder she's so angry about their silence: Dermod's, Gerald's cover-up, and Muriel's silence too. She's angry with Muriel as well as with Dermod. It didn't occur to me that Mary Anne hadn't known for years and years. [Mary Anne told me, subsequently, that her aunt Brigid had in fact told her about the half-sister many years previously.] This recently acquired and painful knowledge must lie behind Mary Anne's cryptic references not just to silent families but also to destructive mothers. The existence of Dermod's illegitimate child is for me a fact like any other in the biographical story, something I learned about without emotion. But not of course for Mary Anne. I feel I've failed to exercise sufficient empathy – and imagination. This is my research, but it is Mary Anne's life.

I talked this over with Mon. When Mary Anne was telling me about her half-sister, should I have let on that I knew already because her mother had told me? No, said Mon decisively. I think she's probably right. The fact that Muriel had told me might have made Mary Anne even more furious with her mother than she already was.

Why did Muriel tell me, I wonder? Perhaps because she'd recently discussed it with Mary Anne and had been upset by Mary Anne's strong and angry reaction? (I don't know if this is how Mary Anne reacted. She may have hidden her feelings from her mother.) By telling me (and I just happened to be the next person who came along who knew, or was interested in, all the people involved) Muriel was in a way normalizing it. She could be confident that I would have no other reaction beyond professional interest.

Or am I much more implicated? Was it precisely because of my intrusion into their lives that this has come to light, so hurtfully to Mary Anne?

And did secretive Rose know about Dermod's illegitimate unacknowledged baby, half-sister to her own goddaughter? I wonder. I imagine that she did; very probably she knew of it some considerable time before Muriel herself was informed.

4 February

I woke up in the middle of last night convinced by a dream that Gerald (and it was his first name only in the dream, not Gerald O'Donovan) had deliberately held back his career as a writer, stepped aside, so as to be able instead to encourage and support Rose.

5 February

With my eldest child coming up to eighteen I've been reflecting on how I have never had less money of my own in my adult life than I have now. I'm giving a talk in Bridgwater on Wednesday for which I hope to get £75 (or is it only £50?) which could take us out for a birthday meal. I know a successful life is measured in more than financial terms, but even so ... am feeling depressed by it.

23 February

I rang Jane, Mary Anne's younger sister, about ten days ago, asking if I could come and talk to her about her godmother Marjorie Grant Cook – I'd just been reading MGC's strange and moving French-Canadian anguished mother-love novel *Another Way of Love*, and also the Canadian childhood scenes of *The Velvet Deer*, that Mary Anne had lent me – and Jane sounded perfectly friendly on the phone, told me there were a couple of paintings MGC had given her that she would show me etc. Then yesterday I received a letter: 'I am sorry but I have decided not to meet you to talk about my godmother. I will not change my mind.'

5 March

To southern Ireland for three days with Mum and Dad, to Ballymaloe, an old country house now a hotel. For three days the sun shone, on the glittering Atlantic and the snow covered Galtee mountains and on the brightly painted houses of the little market towns we drove through on our way up towards Limerick, through Caher and Tipperary and Oola, to find Abington Rectory, where our distant relation Joseph Sheridan Le Fanu had stones thrown at him, when he and his brother were children, by angry Catholic peasants. When they weren't dodging the bailiffs, that is. We found it, and the Le Fanu stone slab in the – mixed – graveyard ... arh, it's not like that now, see, we're all here together, said Catholic John Dee, local historian, who gave us a big hand and asked Dad to sign a couple of Le Fanu books.

At Ballymaloe I found in the bookshelves a copy of *Bowen's Court*, Elizabeth Bowen's story of her beloved ancestral home, which was torn down by the farmer she sold it to in 1960. She should have done what so many of the impoverished gentry have done and turned it into a hotel. Also a book on the Yeats sisters which talked about Father Jeremiah O'Donovan commissioning embroidered banners from Lily Yeats for the redecoration of Loughrea Cathedral. And how W B Yeats interfered between Lily and his brother Jack who had designed some of them. That's the first time I've come across O'Donovan in a secondary source.

Email from Mary Anne this morning: her sister is prone to depressions and withdrawals, and I shouldn't take personally her refusal to see me or talk to me. I feel relieved, and very grateful to Mary Anne who, it now occurs to me, has proved herself considerably more sensitive to my feelings than I am to hers.

Why should any of the O'Donovans talk to me? They must be fed up to the back teeth with people nosing into their family stories: first Constance, then Jane Emery, and now me.

I dreamed last night that I was standing outside a bookshop in a narrow lane of half-timbered houses, with stepped alleyways running between them – I think it was somewhere in Germany. I was waiting for the bookshop to open. I'd written a collection of stories called *Dreaming of Black Rats*. Or it might have been *The Dreaming of Black Rats*.

5 April

Massive teaching effort last weekend for the University's Access Unit. It ran from Thursday evening to Monday lunchtime: autobiography and family history for blind and visually impaired students. This time we were very careful not to leave anyone behind when we had an excursion to the theatre. Our evening outing took us to the Bristol Old Vic and an Asian musical adapted from a Bollywood film. After some tiresome non-cooperation from the front-of-house staff, we filled the front row. You could see surprise written on the actors' faces when they took their curtain call, bowing, eyes cast down, noticing for the first time a row of sleeping guide dogs in the well at their feet. I got home Monday lunchtime feeling like a wrung-out dishrag, the phone rang, and on the other end I heard a depressed-sounding woman from the Arts Council, saying she was ringing about the Writers' Awards. I thought, 'She's going to say she's sorry, I haven't been successful,' and simultaneously I realised that she wouldn't ring me up to tell me that – she would write a letter instead. Just as I thought all this she said, 'I'm very pleased to tell you that you've won an award.' Well! It is just fantastic. And sort of out of the blue as I'd quite given up thinking about it. £7,000, and a panel of writers – Jim Crace, Carol Ann Duffy, Maya Jaggi – who like my second chapter, the Varazze chapter, and consider my book worthy of an award.

I couldn't possibly come to London the next day to have my photograph taken, could I? Well, of course I could! I'd happily go to John O'Groats. Anything she asked I would say yes to. It just so happened, I told her, that I was coming up for my mother's birthday. So up I went on my GWR special offer £10.00 return, and went first to the Arts Council building in Victoria, up to the 25th floor, where the depressed-voice woman was there with a photographer – a fashion photographer, no less. Who are the other writers? I asked. She wouldn't say. We were being hustled in and out of the building without being allowed to catch sight of each other – pity I hadn't squinted at the list at reception.

All meant to be deadly secret until June. I told Michèle (of course), and also told her that Diana Hendry and Tom Pow had both won Scottish Book Awards, not knowing until I had a further conversation with Diana later that that too was meant to be a deadly secret.

I can now afford to go to Trebizond.

26 April

A letter from Muriel Thomas yesterday enclosing some newspaper clippings of obituaries of Rose which she is offering, I must conclude, as propitiation, or as a valedictory gift, in return for saying that Rose's letters to her, Muriel – the five or six she mentioned – could be of no interest to me, that she's discussed this with Mary Anne, and please not to use her name in the book. In other words: Goodbye. I don't know what to think. Mary Anne was so forthcoming to me, so generous with papers and with books, that it seems odd that she should advise Muriel to have nothing more to do with me. Is it that it has just taken the O'Donovans a bit of time to recognize, or to realize, that they feel uneasy and insecure about a stranger rooting through their family history? That seems to me quite likely. I mean I can imagine feeling the same: initially you're forthcoming, you welcome the biographer into your home, perhaps you're a little bit flattered by her interest, or perhaps you have a particular point of view (of Gerald? of Beryl?) you'd like to express; then you become uneasy, perhaps you're being reminded of stuff you'd rather not remember, perhaps you don't like the idea of what your mother, or your sister, or your daughter might say. Perhaps you said a bit too much. Perhaps you have said enough.

Is it coincidental that Mary Anne's mother and sister have decided to stop talking to me (or decided not to begin, in the sister's case) just when I start asking questions about Marjorie Grant Cook? It strikes me as odd that I've drawn a blank on her. Odd in that she was a published writer and, according to Muriel, smart, flamboyant and glamorous. But where is she in everyone's reminiscences? And why doesn't Muriel want her own name in the book, considering she's already mentioned in Jane Emery's book?

Perhaps unfairly, or even absurdly, I feel hurt by this rejection.

Lisa Tuttle rang. She's on the panel for the Arthur C Clarke award. We talked about China Miéville and *Perdido Street Station*. What a good title. Lisa thinks it counts as fantasy rather than SF because of all the magic in it. But if it's future/alternate London then doesn't that place it in the SF camp? I'll try and go to the Awards ceremony. The last time I went I had a baby strapped on my back. It was fifteen, fifteen!! years ago. Then I got a phone call from Hannah Kanter, friend from my early days at The Women's Press. She's just started reading Iris Murdoch's *Under the Net* for the first time, in a 1955 edition, and she read out to me from the back cover a lovely piece by Iris about herself which appears beneath a glamorous author photograph. Iris's husband John Bayley in the books he's written about her since she died allows her no glamour, no sexual charm.

><•>

27 April

I've booked tickets for Turkey for September. Mon's going to take time off work and come with me. To the Towers of Trebizond!

><•>

3 May

New journal: plain, shiny black cover, bought from the Post Office. After weeks of putting it off I eventually tackled the catalogue cards sent from the Harry Ransom Research Centre, which I'd left untouched on the far corner of my desk because they looked so difficult to deal with, along with the forms to fill out for permission to read Rose's letters, which I'd eventually managed to download from the HRRC website. Although it took me a whole day it proved not nearly as difficult as I had thought it would be.

I'm kicking myself for not dashing up to Muriel's flat the moment she told me she'd got those five or six letters from Rose, banging on her door and demanding to read them there and then, rather than politely hanging back and waiting for her to suggest a convenient time. Thank God I spent that whole day at Mary Anne's reading the correspondence between Dermod and Gerald. Who knows? Perhaps I won't be allowed back there. Another lesson learned: grab people before they change their minds about talking to you and showing you their letters. Don't hang about!

><•>

9 May

Harriet Harvey Wood, who used to run the British Council's literature department, alerted me to the existence of the WATCH file at the University of Reading (writers' copyright details gathered in association with the Harry Ransom Centre). She must think me an absolute idiot for not already knowing about it. However I found no reference to Marjorie Grant Cook under any of the names that I know she used: Marjorie Grant/Marjorie Grant Cook/Caroline Seaford. Am I quite mad to be spending so much time pursuing her? But I emailed the man in charge of the WATCH file and he emailed back to say he'd wandered upstairs to where the library keeps their Jonathan Cape archive, and had found in it one letter from Caroline Seaford. Do authors who publish under pseudonyms usually sign their letters pseudonymously, I wonder, if they're corresponding with people who know their real names? Did novelist Mary Kingsley sign her letters Lucas Malet? I might go and have a look at it.

✒

11 May

All week I have been thinking about and reading around the 1920s chapter. The usual range of emotions, from excitement to fear. I don't know where to start. Rose was at the height of her fame (and fortune?): she published eight novels between 1920 and 1930, six of them in the first six years of the decade. Apart from *Towers*, which must be the book for which she's now best-known, her next best-known books I think all come from that six-year period: *Dangerous Ages*, *Told by an Idiot*, *Crewe Train*.

I remember how astonished I was when I discovered that those weren't Rose's first novels; that she had already published nine or ten books, starting way back in 1906.

Perhaps I should use that line from the poem in *Three Days* as the chapter title – an earnest, grown-up, working woman? Self-mocking as usual. It's an appealing characteristic of hers. And she satirises the whole book-writing, news-reading, thought-thinking, views-holding world so brilliantly in *Crewe Train*. I love the dinner party scene when poor Denham asks Arnold what she should talk about, and he airily recommends talking about something she's seen, or heard, or a book she's read. The only book Denham's recently read is a book on dog diseases, so she asks the young man next to her at table: Have you ever had a dog with kidney disease? And he flashes back: No, but I have a goldfish with acute neurosis.

Marjorie Grant Cook didn't publish a novel after 1923 until she re-surfaced as Caroline Seaford ten years later. So it wasn't just Gerald who stopped writing when Rose was flying from success to success in the early 20s.

><•

23 May

On Saturday evening I went to the Arthur C Clarke awards in the Science Museum. It was won by China Miéville for *Perdido Street Station*, by chance the only book on the shortlist I'd managed to read. Of course I was really pleased as I felt as if I'd been championing it, which I had, but only by default as it were. China was shaven-headed, pierced, ringed and tattooed, and guarded by a posse of beautiful people. He gave a good acceptance speech about what an honour it was to be on a shortlist with so many excellent SF writers. Later the critic Farah Mendlesohn who is curvy and cuddly and sexy came up and introduced herself and told me that *In the Chinks of the World Machine* had changed the nature of science fiction criticism, that obviously I had no idea how important I was 'to a whole generation' of critics, and that I was 'like a god to her'. I could hardly believe my ears. What? And what again? Sweet, sweet honey. She insisted that many other people felt the same way, took me by the hand and introduced me left and right – 'and this is Sarah LeFanu' – to people to whom I'm sure I'm not 'like a god', but who nonetheless smiled politely and shook me by the hand. Earlier I had failed to find the pub where I was meant to be meeting up with Lisa Tuttle and Robert Holdstock, so instead I'd dashed along to Princes Gardens, just up from the Science Museum, to look at number 44, where Rose rented a room from Naomi Royde-Smith in 1921 or thereabouts, and where for a year or two they held evening soirées (with other 'South Kensington riff raff', according to Ms Snooty Woolf) – but number 44 has fallen to the concrete and glass of Imperial College. I met up with Lisa and Rob in the Museum, by which time I was light-headed with Farah's extraordinary praise. When I told Christopher Priest (ex-husband of Lisa) that I'd won an Arts Council award he congratulated me and generously told me that he'd often applied for one but had always been turned down.

I spent Monday in the British Library reading Marjorie Grant Cook's First World War novel – her first novel, I think – *Verdun Days in Paris*.

25 May

R H Macaulay, Rose's uncle Regi, at Kirnan, his estate in Argyll, bred a rock plant which was named after him: *gentiani macaulayi*. I've put Lisa on the case (I'm not actually sure how close her home in Tarbert is to Kirnan) to find out more about Kirnan if she can.

5 June

I might use some extracts from his novel *Waiting* as an introduction to the chapter on Gerald. Strong powerful stuff on the corruptibility of priests. Is Maurice Blake, like Father Ralph, a partial self-portrait?

6 June

Martin Amis in *Experience*: never start consecutive paragraphs with the same word, unless you do so deliberately. Also: biographers should always say what their subjects are reading, as it's indicative of states of mind. What's interesting with Rose Macaulay too is what her characters are reading.

8 June

Nicholas Albery, editor of the wonderful *Poem for the Day* anthology, was killed in a car crash, aged only 52. In the paper there's a lovely picture of him smiling beneath a wide-brimmed summer hat.

11 June

The money has come at last. At last! It wasn't in this morning's post, and I was so disappointed that I blurted out to the postman that I was expecting a cheque from the Arts Council. He promised that if anything arrived for me in the 11 o'clock delivery he would bring it over from the sorting office. At 11.45 I set off across the moor to the station to get advance tickets for going to London on Wednesday for the award ceremony at the National Portrait Gallery, worried that buying the tickets might push me over my overdraft limit – and there was the postman, speeding towards me in his van, with an envelope addressed to me on the seat beside him ... Good old postie!

><

22 June

A week has passed since my moment of triumph at the awards ceremony. Hanging around outside the National Portrait Gallery waiting for the doors to open – having just nipped round the corner to see the new Rachel Whiteread sculpture of a plinth on the fourth plinth in Trafalgar Square – I saw a man wandering up and down with a woman and teenage girl in tow, who looked familiar but I just couldn't think who he was. The doors opened and everyone surged in, and I found myself next to Pete Ayrton of Serpent's Tail.

'D'you know who's won an award?' asks Pete.

'Apart from me, no.'

Pete's look of astonishment was fleeting; he at once composed his face to express delight on my behalf. Later on, he said it was a tribute to the Arts Council that it would give an award to writers as diverse as myself and Stewart Home – who, being an ex-author of Pete's, needless to say writes about sex, drugs and men dismembering women.

'Diverse'. I just love Pete.

My agent Judith Murray turned up to cheer for me in a shocking pink dress and matching bangles and everybody had a jolly time with scant respect paid to the portraits on the walls. Salman Rushdie spoke eloquently and humorously about how he'd been given a grant of £7,500 in 1981 when he was writing *Shame* and how it kept him for six months when he was penniless and unknown – and about the new prize for fiction set up in memory of his late wife (ex-wife) Clarissa. By then I'd discovered that the man whom I thought I knew was Matthew Barton, poet, friend of Philip Lyons, who did a joint reading with Philip

7. Sarah LeFanu receiving an Arts Council Award from Salman Rushdie,
June 2001. Photo by Richard H Smith.

for my blind and visually impaired course two or three years ago. He
was first up (coming at the beginning of the alphabet) to shake Salman's
hand and receive the envelope. We each had our photos taken standing
beside Salman, while everybody clapped. It was incredibly exciting.
Michael Horovitz hove into view, weighed down by plastic bags bulging
with copies of *New Departures*, looking the same, if a trifle thinner, as
when I last saw him years ago. There was much drinking and canapé-
eating, except by Salman's bodyguards, who stood so frozen-faced
they too might have been portraits in bronze or plaster.

Now I just have to write the book.

At the A Level art show on Monday, I'm spotted by the headmaster
as he walks past the classroom window. He stops, turns back and says

something I can't catch. I try to open the window but it's locked. He takes his wallet out of his jacket, opens it, and waves a £5.00 note at me. Money, he mouths, grant ... How did you hear? I shout. People are staring. I don't know what they think of the headmaster waving money at me through the window. '*Bristol Evening Post*,' he mouths. Sure enough, in the *Post*, Matthew and I are 'promising writers', who have received a 'handout'. Forty-seven may seem a bit old to qualify as a promising writer – but better than not being a promising writer at all.

Chapter Eight: July–August 2001

Home/Reading/Wales/Lake District/Brighton/Home

1 July

I wrote to Francis King to ask if I could go and talk to him about Rose. I had just read *The Ants' Colony* – ex-pats and English teachers in post-war Florence, a homage to E M Forster. Apparently he has written a biography of Forster. He was a friend of eccentric Ivy Compton-Burnett and Margaret Jourdain, and that's how he met Rose. I was just thinking yesterday that although he's written over twenty novels he never seems to have been much in the public eye, and then I turned on the radio and who should be one of Ned Sherrin's guests? Francis King.

An excellent day in Reading last week: long-haired Michael Bott was very helpful with the WATCH register, on which he was one of the original scholars. I read the Rose Macaulay/Leonard Woolf correspondence, which reveals Rose as the ultimate author from hell. She would sign a contract that included US rights, and promptly promise the same rights to another publisher, leaving Leonard Woolf to sort it out; she 'couldn't remember' delivery dates; she would demand that Woolf send her proofs to places all over Italy and Sicily, places from which she had already departed. Please would Mr Woolf sort out the index to *Some Religious Elements* and check everyone's name?; sorry, she's 'forgotten' to write the bits on E M Forster's unpublished novel that she'd promised to write, so she'll add them when she gets the proofs. And so on. Leonard Woolf must have had the patience of a saint – and the courtesy of a gentleman.

I discovered that Rose had wanted her second book for Hogarth to be on 'supernaturalism' in literature rather than on religion in literature, and had argued strongly for it – but had to bow to Leonard Woolf, who said 'supernaturalism' would be too restrictive. I put off reading *Some Religious Elements* for ages precisely because of its dreary-sounding title. Had it been called 'Supernatural Elements in ...' I feel sure I would have read it ages ago.

Marjorie Grant Cook's 'Caroline Seaford' letter to Jonathan Cape gossips to him about the Reverend Kilvert's predilection for little girls, and (just like Rose's letters to John Murray) rubbishes her own latest novel – by which I think she must mean *They Grew in Beauty*, which came out in 1946. She promises Mr Cape that her next novel will contain neither piety nor pregnancy. (What happened to it? As far as I can tell *They Grew in Beauty* was her last published novel.)

And, oh joy, almost all the letters were in typescript. I have peeked, only, at the parcel from the Harry Ransom Centre: a dismaying amount of almost illegible handwriting.

><

13 July

Out of the blue flew a letter from Muriel Thomas yesterday: MGC's literary executor was 'a Mrs Sybil Challoner, probably now deceased.' Now what? Hmm.

Francis King said at first there was no point in us meeting up as his and Rose's lives 'barely touched', but he eventually gave in. I'm learning the biographer's art of bullying. I'm reading his book – nicely written of course – on E M Forster. He said to me on the phone that he didn't know why Rose didn't mention EMF's homosexuality in her book on him; she was too 'sophisticated', he said, not to know of it (unlike Lionel Trilling, to whom it came as a nasty shock), but perhaps she didn't want to offend him. But to mention it surely would have laid EMF open to criminal charges? Rose was being necessarily discreet.

><

Tŷ Newydd

Only one noticeably disturbed student on the course, keen to prove at every opportunity that she herself is a writer and teacher and better in many if not most ways than Michèle Roberts or me. Yesterday morning, while I was still in bed, and Michèle was making coffee in the kitchen, we were talking through the open door about how difficult this woman was to deal with in the workshops. I got out of bed to pick up a pile of students' manuscripts from the table and spotted a figure just outside my bedroom window, bending over, apparently picking up stones and peering at them, not five feet from where I was standing. I froze for a second, then tiptoed into the kitchen and whispered, there's someone outside my window, and I think it might be ... Michèle peered round the door – no, no, it couldn't be the woman we'd just been loudly discussing, but hang on, yes, oh my god, it is her .... Very unnerving. I kept my window locked tight last night just in case. Otherwise a good bunch of students with five or six serious writers including Lynn Kramer and beautiful Jenny Newman who is always wonderful to have in a group as she's reliably good and helps stabilise the flighty ones.

Jackie Kay came last night and gave a generous, accomplished and powerful reading.

We talked a lot with Jenny about convents and spiritual hunger. I've only quite recently read her brilliant but disturbing novel *Going In*, which of course – I now realize – draws on her own experiences as a novice in the 1960s. On the last day Sally's Elis turned up at our little cottage brandishing a brace of lobsters; we've been teasing him for years about providing us with lobsters from his pots out in the bay, and this time he really did it. So we took them round to Jenny's where we'd been invited to drink Martini, and ate them there with Jenny and Lynn, and then first Sally turned up in search of one of us, and then Elis turned up in search of Sally, so it became quite a party, and I thought of Laurie's cheerful evening at a party with Vere near the end of *The Towers of Trebizond* when they all adapt well-known lines of poetry or prose to suit their friends and acquaintances, and guess who is meant by lines such as 'Lobsters I loved, and after lobsters, sex' (Macaulay 1956, 249).

✦

3 August, Lake District

A couple of days ago I read a review by Charles Spencer, in the *Telegraph*, of a play called *Shagaround*, which he said was a work of energy and genius and humour, and is about four women locking a man into the ladies' lavatory in a pub on New Years Eve. And I thought, oh my god, why are the subjects I'm interested in always so sedate and polite? No wonder Pete Ayrton couldn't believe I'd won the same prize as Stewart Home. I wouldn't know where to start to write a play about four women locking a man in a lavatory. Then Lyn Gardner, in the *Guardian* yesterday, said she had found the play execrable: depressing, mean-spirited, lacking in humour and in political consciousness and any kind of outwardness. That made me feel better!

Last night I dreamt that someone took me to see a publisher, who was first called Mike, then Miles, na Ghopaleen, who was a small left wing/radical publisher like that fellow I used to know at Merlin Press, and a little like Pete Ayrton, and he said I must go away and write my play about Dorothy L Sayers *at once*, and although it might not be a best-seller, he knew publishers in Florence and Poland who would 'snap it up' immediately. Florence and Poland!

Today I drove to Penrith Library where after a fair bit of toing and froing on the microfiche, which always makes me horribly nauseous, I found a notice in the *Westmorland Herald*, 22 July 1939: 'Woman Motorist whose Attention was Diverted'. Emily Macaulay, no less, who said in her defence that her *passenger* had diverted her attention. Rose's (aka Emily's) lawyer asked that her licence should not be endorsed because she was a member of the Women's Voluntary Ambulance Service but the chairman of the Bench did not accept these 'special circumstances' and 'did not see any reason why the licence should not be endorsed as in any other case.'

Sometimes I feel as if I'm treading a well-worn path back towards my subject. Constance gave the details of the accident in her biography thirty years ago, including how Rose blamed her passenger for distracting her while driving. Constance, like Rose, kept Gerald's name out of it. Rose already had form in using her first name Emily in any confrontation with the police over her (lack of) driving skills. Funny that she should have adored driving and yet been so absolutely useless at it. In the 1930s the Gollancz crowd used to make up excuses when she offered to drive them home after late night roistering.

Not that I'm hugely motivated by finding out new 'facts'. I *think* that I think that you don't need new facts in order to get into your subject's heart and mind. But maybe I'm hopeless at it anyway; that if Constance and Jane Emery hadn't performed the groundwork before me I would have completely missed the central relationship of Rose's life. But then I guess I wouldn't be writing it – as I wouldn't have been intrigued by the way her creativity co-existed with the life of her heart. How she avoided convention and domesticity by keeping her heart's life secret.

Just as Dorothy L Sayers did. Sara Davies put forward my drama proposal to the commissioning editors in London and now it's commissioned for Radio 4. It's going to be about DLS giving up her baby, and writing her passion into Lord Peter Wimsey when the men she fell for in 'real' life turned out such losers. But of course I'm relying on other people's detective work (specifically, Barbara Reynolds's) in order to be able to write about these things. I'm going to set it in an advertising office like the one in *Murder Must Advertise* (which DLS based on the place where she first worked in London). They'll all be larking about and filling in crosswords and going out to dance halls in the evenings. It's currently called *Conjunctions*.

Maybe I did discover something new by going to look at the newspaper records in Penrith – I can't remember Constance mentioning the special pleading, nor whether Jane Emery did. Was Rose actually concerned that she wouldn't be able to drive an ambulance? My instinct tells me it was an excuse.

And – of course – who am I kidding? – it would be incredibly exciting to discover something truly new.

><=

21 August: Home

I've just finished typing up the revised script of *Conjunctions*. It's thin and flimsy but I hope that I can fatten it up and make it stronger. I went over to Brighton by train yesterday to meet Gerard Irvine, the young (then) Anglican priest who was friends with Rose in the 1950s. Now, post-stroke, he looks old and tottery, but he was terribly kind. He and his sister Rosemary gave me lunch – pâté, fruit, cheese, salad, all laid out beautifully on a gleaming dining-room table with silverware and nice wine. She's an ex-headmistress, and an ex-pupil of Cheltenham Ladies' College, which brought back some pretty ghastly memories, and led me to dream, last night, of Jane Glendinning, who died at twenty-six or something like that (I hadn't seen her for ten years or more), and whom I remember always with her pale moon face and her pale red hair against those hideous green tweed jackets and skirts we were obliged to wear. The Irvines live in a lovely tall narrow house with iron fretwork balconies in Montpelier Road, which they bought from Francis King thirty years ago against their retirement ('the only sensible thing I ever did,' said Gerard). Rosemary bosses him around in a sisterly way, but left us alone to talk about Rose. She herself related a nice story about Rose driving the two of them to a cocktail party and taking a short cut down a one-way street the wrong way, and pretending to be a frail old lady when stopped by a policeman, so that he escorted them to the end of the road, from which Rose then accelerated away in a cloud of exhaust.

Emails from Polly Gaster and her sister. Their mother was a daughter of Sylvia and Robert Lynd, who were friends of Rose's in the 1930s – but neither of them has any correspondence. Both of them wonder if perhaps their cousin Nancy does.

Elizabeth Sprigge, in *The Life of Ivy Compton-Burnett*, re Rose's death and Ivy's grief at it: 'they were both experts in friendship'. Sprigge's biography can be read as a model of gentility: so-and-so's 'charming house', for example, or the Beresford mother being 'loved for her gentleness', when in fact she had been put away in a mental home by her husband after she'd given birth to five or six children and suffered who knows what humiliations and cruelties. But despite those politenesses and coverings-up, Sprigge is actually very good on Ivy herself and on her novels – more thought-provoking and intriguing, I found, than 'modern' Hilary Spurling, whose hundreds of pages of family analysis left me thinking, 'so what?' Sprigge, in a way, doesn't even try to explain, just gives us: weird family, weird novels. And my god were they all weird. Spurling promises more than she delivers; Sprigge promises much less, but provides generous insights.

Sprigge reproduces a series of three brilliant portrait photos of Ivy C-B as a baby, as a young woman, and as an old woman. They all three look at the world in the same defiant and secretive way. You can see the chubby smiling baby in the unsmiling old woman. Ivy's mad hairstyle – like an upside-down chamber pot, a style to which she remained devoted throughout her life – tends to distract, but they're terrific photos. I'd like to see a similar series of photos of Rose. You can't help but be ghoulishly interested (well, I can't) in the photograph of Ivy with her two sisters who killed themselves, and her adored brother who was killed in the war.

8. Ivy Compton-Burnett. Claude Harris.

Lord Peter Wimsey, in *The Unpleasantness at the Bellona Club*, doesn't find Rose's novels amongst books by the women writers – Dorothy Richardson, May Sinclair, Virginia Woolf and Katherine Mansfield – that Ann Dorland (we're not sure about her at first but she turns out to be basically a good egg) has been reading. But Ann talks to Lord Peter about 'what Rose Macaulay calls "nameless orgies" ...' Does Rose talk about 'nameless orgies' in *Catchwords and Claptrap*? Or is it in *A Casual Commentary*? I think it comes in one of her satirical attacks on the hysteria of the press – so it's probably in *A Casual Commentary* – alongside those brilliant essays on choosing a religion, on keeping house ('a house unkept cannot be so distressing as a life unlived') and on the establishment of the 'unfortunate tradition' that classifies cooking and cleaning as work that specially belongs to women.

Chapter Nine: September 2001

Trabzon, Turkey

Thursday September 6

The internal flight from Istanbul to Trabzon was crammed full of Turks of all shapes and ages: solid middle-aged women in headscarves and loose all-covering robes, accompanied by skinny girls in jeans who were burdened with cardboard boxes tied with string and plastic bags stuffed to bursting; gnarled old men with grey whiskers and beady eyes; strapping young men with sinewy arms and shaven heads. A girl of twelve or thirteen sitting in front of us with two head-scarved older women bobbed up and peered over the back of the seat at me and Mon. 'Hallo. How are you? What is your name?' We told her our names and smiled at her. She giggled. We asked her name. She giggled again and ducked out of sight. When the plane touched down in Trabzon and taxied to a halt the passengers clapped and cheered.

Trabzon

Nearly fifty years on from Rose Macaulay's visit in 1954, which she turned into a novel featuring Laurie, Aunt Dot, Father Hugh Chantry-Pigg, and a highly-strung Bactrian camel. I've lost count of the number of times I've read *The Towers of Trebizond*. I love all the stuff on spying and plagiarism and people pretending to be what they're not. And the way that Rose brings a kind of triumphant (or courageous, perhaps) high-spiritedness to her themes of exile and longing, and love and loss and grief. I think Rose was still haunted by Gerald when she wrote it. She said somewhere to Rosamond Lehmann that *she* felt like a ghost for years after he died, as she makes Laurie feel in *Towers*. And she said that she couldn't not be glad of the past, even if she'd behaved so dishonestly and selfishly. I wonder if I'll find traces of that Rose – loving and clever and hilarious and sad – here, in Trabzon.

Mon has brought a selection of books from the Keele University Turkish collection: two thick volumes, published 1890, of *The Women of Turkey and their Folk-Lore* by Lucy Garnett – perhaps the original of Aunt Dot's projected *Women of the Euxine*? – and *Within the Taurus* by Patrick Kinross. Kinross was in Trabzon in 1951, three years before Rose. He's mentioned in *Towers* as one of Laurie's many friends and acquaintances swanning around Turkey gathering copy for their 'Turkey books'. He describes how once the 'chink of foreign currencies rang through lively, teeming bazaars', in the days when Trebizond was the easternmost town of the Silk Route. But by the 1950s Trabzon was inhabited solely by Turks; and the talk was of the price of hazelnuts. I've been reading Neal Ascherson on the extraordinary mix of tribes and languages and cultures of the Pontic peoples round the Black Sea; the to-ings and fro-ings and killings and settlings and marryings that went on for thousands of years before the mass deportations and the drawing-up of racial boundaries of the twentieth century put an end to it. Before the First World War there were ten thousand Persians in Trebizond, and many more Greeks. The Greeks were all driven out in the *Katastrofe* of 1923.

Under the weight of all these books we staggered down a cobbled lane to a thick wooden door, behind which lies the convent of the one remaining Catholic church in Trabzon, the Sancta Maria Katolika Kilesisi, where we've arranged to stay. It's cheap, and is recommended in the guide book as an alternative to the hotels of Trabzon, some of which, the guide warns, double as brothels. Trabzon is the first biggish town on the road west from the Georgian border, after Hopa and the tea-growing town of Rize, and throughout the 1990s girls have streamed along the road from Georgia and beyond to earn the money they can't earn at home. The guide book calls it 'the Natasha syndrome'.

We have seen no nuns. Quiet-voiced Columba's in charge. She has just acquired a tiny skinny tabby kitten from a Kurdish friend. The undersides of its paws and the surrounding fur are a deep dark black, as if it has just dipped them in the black sand of the Black Sea shore.

We were tired and hungry, and asked Columba where we might find somewhere to eat. Anywhere up on the square, she said, on the *meydan* where the buses and taxis are. It was dark and hot, and we walked up through narrow lanes past men sitting on stools outside their shopfronts, and turned into the *meydan*. And there, looking to my left, I saw a sign – I could hardly believe my eyes – a blazing vertical neon sign saying *Yeşilyurt Otel ve Restaurant*. The Hotel Yessilyurt: where Laurie and Aunt Dot and Father Hugh Chantry-Pigg stay when they arrive in Trabzon; where Laurie finds in her bedside drawer the abandoned manuscript of poor Charles's Turkey book after he has been eaten by a Black Sea shark; the place she returns to alone, after Aunt Dot and Father Chantry-Pigg have slipped over the border behind the Iron Curtain; and where she misreads her Turkish phrase-book and thinks she is saying to the manager, 'I do not understand Turkish,' but in fact is saying, 'Please to phone at once to Mr Yorum'. And Mr Yorum is called and comes down the stairs and bows to Laurie and she feels obliged to buy him a drink and so it goes on for days.

I had imagined myself getting horribly tangled up in tenses as I struggled with my phrase book to formulate, 'Did there use to be a hotel called the Yessilyurt here in Trabzon fifty years ago?' But there it was – bang in the middle of the buildings that make up one side of the central square of Trabzon, its neon sign calling out to me through the hot dark night.

The front door was open and Mon and I went straight in and asked of the man behind the reception desk, 'Restaurant?' He looked surprised, nonplussed, amazed even, but he stood up and politely gestured towards the stairs. At the top he pulled open a frosted glass sliding door and spoke in a low voice to two waiters who were standing inside. They looked at us in surprise, then bowed and waved us in, leading us to a table in a far corner of the pillared dining-room, which seemed to us much too dark a place to be sitting in, so we moved to a more central one, with the waiters scurrying behind us. There seemed to be a lot of women having dinner together; it was noisy and cheerful. An older man, the maitre d', apologised for lack of a menu, but told us what we could have. We said yes to anything, and everything.

We drank thick lentil soup with thin discs of lemon floating on top, and then were served tomato salad with basil, and chicken kebab with long sweet green peppers. It was all freshly-cooked and delicious, and served on crockery decorated with a maroon border and a little crest saying *Yeşilyurt Otel* but chipped and scarred through years of use. Beneath our feet the intricate pattern of the red and yellow carpet was fragmented by threadbare patches like pale islands. Surely the same plates, the same carpet, as when Rose was here inventing Mr Yorum.

9. A plate from the Yeşilyurt Otel, Trebizond, and crest detail.

Revived by hot food and cold beer, Mon and I sat back and looked around us at our fellow-guests: young women with bare midriffs and halter tops, with blonde pony-tails and high shrieks of laughter. It was a bit like being in a girls' school dining-room, or a college refectory when exams were over. 'You don't think these girls could be students, do you?' I asked Mon, or she asked me. And suddenly and simultaneously we realised what should have been obvious to us as soon as we entered the dining-room: our fellow-diners were neither students nor local Trabzon girls. We were surrounded by Natashas from Georgia.

Friday 7 Sept

This morning we set out on a preliminary reconnaissance to find the Towers of Trebizond. Trebizond had become modern Trabzon by the time Rose Macaulay turned up in 1954. She – and her character Laurie – were looking for signs of the Comnenus empire of the thirteenth and fourteenth centuries. 'A lavish but ramshackle empire,' Kinross calls it. The Comneni emperors built a castellated palace on an impregnable ridge of rock tapering to a point high above the shoreline of the Black Sea. In *The Towers of Trebizond* Laurie climbs the broken battlements and scrambles amongst the fallen walls of the ancient palace, straining to hear the ghosts of these emperors and their courtiers and slaves whispering amongst the ruins.

And I'm chasing Rose, straining to catch her whispering. What might I hear about if my ears were attuned to her dry, high-pitched tones? Love, grief, writing, secrets; the tug of history, the folly of the world?

In the *meydan*, where a statue of Kemal Atatürk gazes paternally over the tables and coloured umbrellas of an outdoor café, we hesitated, looking round for somewhere to sit. Most tables were crowded with family groups, and women with shopping bags. About half of the women were headscarved. Rose complained about the women being all muffled up, and said in a letter that she thought it would take fifty years for it to change. There are possibly more headscarves now than there were then, when Atatürk's construction of a modern, secular Turkey was in full swing. As soon as the waiter saw us he went up to a man sitting on his own and told him to get up and sit somewhere else, and waved to us to come and sit down. On the far side of the road, partially obscured by waiting buses, we could see the Yessilyurt by daylight, with its arched windows and a pretty ironwork balcony on the first floor and a semi-circle of patterned marble over the front door.

We ordered tea. I love Turkish tea. I love the little curvy glasses with their delicate red and gold swirls and their lacy metal holders. This must be the very spot, I thought, where Father Chantry-Pigg sets up his portable altar on the feast of Corpus Christi, before processing round the square with a crucifix, to the fury of the local Imam. Rose was seventy-two when she was here, imagining all this. And here I am, chasing her ghost; not the ghost of the little girl she was in Varazze, but the ghost of a complex, secretive, ageing woman, brave, insouciant and alone.

In a way I feel closer to her here than I ever do to her in London, or Cambridge. Is it perhaps easier to glimpse the fleeting figure of your subject across all the intervening years if they themselves are on the move, disconnected, unmoored from their quotidian, as the biographer is from hers? Richard Holmes didn't actually see Robert Louis Stevenson – he was standing on the wrong bridge after all – but he had an overwhelming sense of Stevenson's presence. I wonder if you catch a sense of that presence most strongly when, paradoxically, the subject is away from home; and also when you are.

In *Towers* Aunt Dot orders a taxi to take her and Laurie up to the Citadel. Patrick Kinross had the British Consul's driver take him up there in a jeep. I wished we had had Aunt Dot's sense, or Kinross's diplomatic connections, for we soon learned that if you're on foot and stop to consult a map or guide book, you're at once surrounded by a pressing horde of helpful but hindering Turks. I had been reading in Ascherson about the disastrous government involvement in the Black Sea fishing industry in the 1980s, which resulted in gross overfishing and a consequent destruction of the local economies. Now there's little for the men to do all day except gather round their mosques. Mon and I stopped to get our bearings outside what once was the Byzantine Church of the Golden-Headed Virgin, and is now the Fatih Cami, Mosque of the Conqueror. In a trice we were surrounded by men; two stools and a table were put out on the pavement for us, two glasses of tea procured from inside a nearby doorway, and mutually incomprehensible pleasantries were exchanged as we were urged to drink our tea. Could someone direct us to the ruins of the old palace? No – no – surely we'd like to see inside the Fatih Cami instead?

Twenty minutes later we said our thanks. Mon speaks Farsi, and although Atatürk attempted to prune the language of Persian and other influences, at the same time as he introduced the Roman alphabet in place of Arabic script, there's still enough Persian equivalence to make it not altogether unfamiliar to her. She's already mistress of the formal leave-taking 'Allaha-usmarladuk', and we set off again uphill as if we knew exactly where we were going. By now the sun was high and the road steep. We stopped again and mopped our faces in the shade of a wall. At once three or four more men materialised, stools and a table were set out on the pavement as before, tea (apple tea this time) procured from somewhere, and in no time at all we found ourselves admiring the plain whitewashed interior of another mosque. These men had never heard of a ruined palace here in Trabzon. Might it not be Kemal Atatürk's summer house we really desired to see?

More firm goodbyes, and then, 'Let's ask in that bakery over there,' said Mon. 'Surely a shop assistant won't be able to offer us tea, or take us round a mosque for that matter.'

What a brilliant suggestion. At last we were sent in the right direction back the way we'd come, to a door of thin plywood planks set in a crooked wooden frame that fitted more or less into a hole in a dusty red wall. We had staggered past it unseeing half an hour earlier. We opened the door and walked through and found that at last we were inside the ruined palace of the Comneni emperors. Narrow alleyways snaked between ramshackle houses of wood and brick and corrugated iron that leaned against the thick stone walls. People still lived here, amongst the ruins, just as they did when Rose visited. Frayed trousers and faded shirts dangled from nylon washing lines strung overhead, and chickens ran squawking between our feet. The alleyway opened out, and we passed vegetable patches, a tethered goat, leafy fig trees. Some restoration work had been done on the outer walls, but not much: here and there some blocks of new stone filled the gaps. Above us the red Turkish flag with its white crescent moon and star fluttered high over the battlements, the straight lines of which were broken here and there into crumbling dips and curves. We climbed over rubble, old mortar and brambles to get up to the top of the wall. It's difficult to tell which ruins are which, it's all so ruinous, says Laurie in the novel. And how right she was. We had just identified what we thought might be the castle keep when we saw three small children picking their way in single file towards us along the broken narrow top of the wall: a boy of about eight, a girl of maybe six, and a tiny one tagging behind, dragging a bulging plastic bag.

As the ill-fated Charles says in *Towers*, before he is eaten by a shark and has his Turkey book plagiarised by his erstwhile friend David, 'one can never hope to identify anything while Turks look on' (Macaulay 1956, 42). On the other side of the wall the ground dropped sheer hundreds of feet. This is what made Byzantine Trebizond impregnable. It was now making me and Mon very nervous, especially as regards the tiniest girl, who at that moment allowed her bag to fall and for a moment we were all silent, watching what looked like chipboard and formica offcuts showering down onto the grey rocks a few hundred feet below us. And what with showing them our map, giving the bigger

10. The Byzantine arches in the ruins at Trebizond.

girl the guidebook to carry, telling the boy that no, he couldn't have my camera even if he was threatening to hurl himself over the edge unless I gave it to him, we didn't manage to identify much. It seemed more important to get down off the ramparts before somebody fell off, and so we allowed our guides to lead us down through the washing lines strung across the narrow pathways and past the hovels, one of which was doubtless their home. We left them with the map and a little bit of money, and resolved to come back quietly on Monday, when we hoped they might be at school.

Rose's imagination must have been at the peak of its powers when she saw the heart of the Comnenus empire amidst this tumbled masonry. Mon and I agreed that neither of us had sensed the ghosts of an ancient civilisation.

Back in the *meydan*, we stopped outside a restaurant on the eastern side to look at the menu. At once a uniformed man sprang up at our side, *Polis* written on his shirt, introduced himself as Tourism Police, and told us this was a good restaurant for us, as the restaurants on the other side of the square – he gestured towards the Yessilyurt – had Russian women, and we would not want to eat with Russian women. Bad women. Women in Turkey, he went on, did not eat alone. This restaurant was good for us women, he said, because it was secret. We acquiesced. Not only did the meze taste as if it was days old, but we were the only women there and were made to feel considerably more conspicuous and unwelcome than in the Yessilyurt.

Saturday September 8

Today we cunningly wrote down our planned route on a slip of paper which we could glance at on the hoof, thereby avoiding helpful Turkish men and enforced mosque visits. In the morning we took a *dolmuş* – a shared taxi: the taxi advertises its destination and you get in and wait until the other two or three seats are taken, then off you go at breakneck speed – up to the top of Boz Tepe, a hill to the south east of the town that was once sacred to Mithras. Soldiers were doing exercises behind barbed wire. We sat in a dilapidated tea-garden below the army base, on a little roofed dais with peeling blue railings, and drank tea and ate bread and yoghourt and looked out over the town and harbour and tried to identify the old walled city and the Comneni ruins. But even without Turks looking on it was pretty difficult, and the view was obscured by overgrown larches.

In the afternoon we took another *dolmuş* out to the Byzantine church of Aya Sofya, where Laurie sat on the camel outside the south porch below a relief frieze of scenes from Genesis and pondered the crumbling figures of Adam and Eve and the serpent, and the inscription in Greek which is something to do with sin and forgiveness. I suspect Rose got the translation out of Lynch or Murray or another of her nineteenth century Trebizond experts. It's difficult enough to make out the letters, let alone translate them. I have been noticing a tendency in myself to elide Rose with her creation, Laurie. In the novel Laurie translates the Greek as she's sitting there on the camel. No, I don't believe it. The Comnenus eagle spreads its stone wings up at the top of the arch. Aya Sofya was used for years as a military store; a photograph in Kinross's book shows barrels piled up against the closed porch doors.

Inside, black pigeons flew in and out of the arched windows high up in the dome and settled on a ledge at the feet of a host of golden angels swirling round a serene enthroned Virgin. In *Towers* Aya Sofya is quiet and solitary enough for Laurie to meditate on sin (in general) and adultery (in particular), but now it's surrounded by new housing, and blasted by the din of diggers digging up the sea shore and lorries grinding along the coast road carrying enormous lumps of black rock.

We ate again in the Yessilyurt. The atmosphere was different. We think that Thursday night must have been the Natashas' night off. Now we observed more drinking, less eating: lots of little groups of two or three girls scattered round the tables, more make-up, fewer pony-tails, each group clustering round a man, all of them, as far as we could see without staring too obviously, middle-aged men in dark suits. They looked like businessmen. I guess they were businessmen: checking the goods before making their purchase.

The manager welcomed us courteously. And if anyone else thought our presence peculiar, they were too polite to show it. Or perhaps eccentric English women have become a Yessilyurt tradition, one started by Rose Macaulay.

Laurie weaves an exotic romance around her picture of Circassian slave girls at the Comnenus court. It would be hard to romanticise the lives of these girls. What would Aunt Dot have thought, with all her grand plans for the liberation of the women of the Euxine?

> ●

Sunday 9 Sept

We booked ourselves onto a tour bus to Sumela, the 'monastery in the clouds'. Rose didn't do this, but we thought it would be crazy to miss the opportunity. You couldn't get to it when she was here; even Patrick

Kinross in the Consul's jeep, and sustained with sandwiches packed by the Consul's wife, was forced to turn back. Anyway, the road from Trabzon ran up beside what I thought was probably the River Pyxitis, at the mouth of which the 10,000 men of Xenophon's army were given intoxicating honey by the Trapezuntines. Laurie often thinks about the 'madding honey', and she fishes in the Pyxitis, too. It's got another name now, and I knew it would be useless to ask Ömer, our tour guide, if it was the classical River Pyxitis. Instead I asked if there were fish in it. 'No, no fish,' he declared. We turned a corner and came upon a group of four or five men busy catching fish.

'Can I be tourist guide in England?' Ömer asked us. 'What languages must I speak?' Mon told him we had a lot of Japanese tourists. 'Japan? I hate the Japan! And I hate the French! You know why I hate the French?' No, we didn't know why. 'Because French say that we killed Armenians. We didn't kill Armenians. I hate Armenians.' He paused, then, 'Greeks. You know Greeks? We have some Greeks in Trabzon. They change their names and speak Turkish, but *we know they are Greeks*.' I gazed out of the coach at the Pyxitis, and tried to conjure up Xenophon and his ten thousand marching down the valley. Mon meanwhile had opened the guidebook at a chart showing the Greek and Armenian population of Trabzon in the nineteenth century as numbering over twelve thousand and recklessly (I thought) showed this to Ömer.

There were six other tourists with us: two young Czech couples who had been walking in the Kaçkar Mountains, and a twenty year old student from Istanbul on holiday with her mother. Later we were grateful to the mother for slowing the pace as we toiled up through the beech trees and azaleas and dripping black pines towards the monastery, with the clouds flying up the valley like smoke, parting now and again to reveal a terrifyingly sheer drop and trees like knots of rope twisting out from the further cliff face. Ömer wanted us under his thumb. He'd forgotten Mon's name, so he kept barking at me, if he thought we were dawdling: 'Sarra, come here now, with your friend!' This amused the Czechs no end. 'Kitchen department one,' said Ömer, herding us into one small room. 'Kitchen department two, Sarra, come here now!' herding us into the next. 'Kitchen department three,' said one of the Czech boys, amidst snorts of laughter, as we trooped into another crudely renovated room. 'Sarra, come here now, with your friend!' We viewed a smoke-blackened ceiling and were not surprised to hear Ömer blame the Greek monks for the ruination of their own monastery. Mon pointed out to me the graffiti on some of the frescoes, graffiti that's over a hundred years old. She said you could see similar in Iran. Some of it was in Greek. Neal Ascherson calls the ruins of Sumela 'hate-ruins' rather than 'time-ruins'.

We came down in pouring rain, and at the restaurant at the foot of the mountain were invited by Taler, the student, and her mother to join them at their table. They helped us order local dishes, which turned out to be melted cheese with flour, melted cheese with flour with an egg in it, and melted cheese with flour inside an omelette with a tiny bit of anchovy. We hoped it wasn't part of what had been the last remaining anchovy in the Black Sea.

'I am like an ice,' said Ömer plaintively as we climbed on to the coach. The Czechs looked at each other and sniggered.

Back in Trabzon we braved the Yessilyurt with a speech I had laboriously prepared in Turkish the night before. I read it out to the manager: 'I am writing a book about this woman' (pointing to a photo of Rose on the back of a paperback edition of *The Towers of Trebizond*). 'She stayed in the Yessilyurt Hotel fifty years ago. Please may I buy a souvenir, for example, a plate?' At first, like Mr Yorum when summoned in error by Laurie, he looked politely puzzled, until I reached the third sentence, when he rushed off, and returned moments later with a plate with the crimson Yessilyurt crest on it, which he pressed into my hands and refused all attempts at payment. It was the first unchipped plate we'd seen, but the glaze was deeply scored by maybe fifty years of knives and forks. Possibly a plate that Rose herself had eaten off. We said our thanks and goodbyes and turned to go, just as two Natashas slipped up the stairs behind us to the second floor.

Monday 10 Sept

We crept back into the ruins, whispering so that our three small erstwhile companions wouldn't know we were there. We clambered up on to the ramparts once more. Amidst the numerous broken internal walls I suddenly saw the two arches containing the pointed windows separated by thin stone columns that Laurie claims as the windows of the Emperors' banqueting hall, through which she looks down over the ruined outer walls to the ravine and the western bay of Trebizond. I hadn't recognised them before because it was just at that very point that the little boy had threatened to hurl himself into the abyss, and we had had to hurry down to firmer ground. Laurie of course has the advantage of exploring the ruins with a copy of the floor plan that Charles had filched for his book, uncredited, from the explorer H F B Lynch: 'now that poor Charles was in purgatory,' she muses, 'no doubt he was learning to be more truthful' (Macaulay 1956, 155).

It was at this spot, right beneath the Byzantine windows, that Laurie sells all Aunt Dot's pills and mixtures to a Greek sorcerer for eight kurus and a bottle of green liquid. When she drinks from the bottle she's transported into the ancient Comneni palace, and sees silk-clothed courtiers and disputing ecclesiastics and a young man playing chess with an ape and Circassian slave girls and two young princes having their eyes put out in a palace revolution.

A young woman with shining brown hair, bare feet, and wearing a checkered pinafore over the full skirts of her brown dress, approached us on the dusty red path: these are my trees, she said, or we guessed she said, gesturing at a small tangle of fig trees and hazel growing in earth once covered (if my calculations were right) by the inlaid marble floor of the banqueting hall. Come, she beckoned us. We followed her down a narrow alleyway round the foot of the keep, where we squeezed past a potbellied man on a low wooden stool, his face hidden behind a newspaper. The woman stopped by an open doorway set into the wall, and scooped out a handful of hazelnuts from the large hairy sack propped against it. She tossed them one by one into her mouth, cracking them merrily in her strong-looking white teeth, and laughed as she talked. She cupped our hands in hers, and poured a heap of nuts into them. Nervously I cracked one between my back teeth. She laughed at our anxious expressions, and picked the nuts from our hands to crack them open for us. Behind Mon's shoulder another woman appeared out of the alleyway – small and wrinkled, but bearing a strong resemblance to the younger woman; and at almost the same time, framed in a window opening into a low dark room, hidden deep inside the palace walls, appeared another woman: ancient, toothless, smiling and waving a welcome. She looked old enough to have been living there half a century ago at least, while Rose Macaulay was scrambling about on the ruined ramparts above, dreaming of lost glories and empires turned to dust and chasing her vision of the fabled city with its shimmering, unreachable towers. Perhaps, I thought, in those days this toothless crone had been married to a Greek sorcerer. Who knows? And had, herself, offered a handful of sweet hazelnuts to the lean Englishwoman as she dropped from the ramparts onto the sandy red path that led past her doorway.

Chapter Ten: October–December 2001

Home/London/Home

3 October

Since returning from Turkey I've written up two versions of the trip: one for the *Arvon Journal* and one for a twenty minute slot on Radio 3, which Sara Davies, wonderfully, has managed to get commissioned. Meanwhile I've skirted round picking up the pieces of the 1930s chapter. How to get back into it after so long away from it? I have been reading Rose's *Milton* over the last few days: perhaps the chapter could focus on Rose as a biographer ...? She is present in both the Milton book and in *The Writings of E M Forster*, not in a heavy-handed way, but in a light, modern way that's mediated through an awareness of her own subjectivity. Perhaps that could be the core of the chapter?

I have also spent quite a lot of time skirting round – or rather avoiding doing anything about – the correspondence that's been copied for me and sent by the Harry Ransom librarian. It has become what I think people call a locus of anxiety. What's my problem with it? I think it has been contaminated by William's brutal assertion that my book isn't sufficiently scholarly to merit a British Academy grant and doesn't add to the sum of human knowledge. I keep on picking up the package and riffling through it, and then putting it down again. Almost, I suppose, as if I might find something in it that I don't want to.

22 October

The biographies of Milton and Forster haven't become *the* core of the next chapter, but, perhaps, if it's possible to have more than one core, *a* core. I've divided the chapter into histories – *Some Religious Elements in English Literature* and *They Were Defeated* (1931 and 1932) – and then move on to *Milton* (1934) and biographies. Now I have to somehow tuck in everything else, that is, everything that Rose was *doing* (besides writing). I think this is what a biography is meant to be: a folding-in of all the ingredients, the living, the loving, the writing, to make a rich pudding. Oh dear. And reading Alison Light on Englishness and conservatism between the wars, I'm worried about not dealing in this chapter with what she talks about so interestingly, that is, modernism. Although I think her view of 'Edwardian' as being all fusty and repressed is perhaps a bit monolithic.

❤

23 October

Francis King emailed me yesterday to say sorry, but he doesn't really have time to meet me and talk about Rose. He said that as he gets older more and more people ask to meet him because he was acquainted with this or that now-famous dead person and everyone else who knew them except him is also dead. I sympathise – blimey I try and put off strangers who want to come and talk to me about *In the Chinks of the World Machine* – in fact I have become positively averse to meeting strangers and try to put off everyone who isn't an old friend. And I'm barely half Francis King's age. So I'll tell him that that's fine and not to worry. While I was thinking last night about what I had wanted to talk to him about, viz Rose's biography of E M Forster, and how she at once identifies with, and values, Forster's sense of his own position on the periphery (his homosexuality/her femaleness), but at the same time is envious of his place at King's, right at the heart of the literary academical establishment, I suddenly thought I could put *Cambridge* at the heart of the 1930s section: her ambivalent yearning for a place of privilege from which she is excluded. Cambridge is there as a locus of desire – a dangerous and finally fatal desire – in *They Were Defeated*, and is central to *Milton*. In *The Writings of E M Forster* Rose seems to be coming to terms with her ambivalence, and at the same time, perhaps because of that, she's recognizing that Cambridge is not really the centre of the world after all. She sees that there's a much wider world, which is about to come crashing down around everyone's ears.

Rose's 1930s are stuffed with friends, journalism, broadcasting, and all the places abroad where she's setting her novels, but these three books explore her investment in Cambridge as a home for heart and mind. I think this would be more effective than the current awkward histories/biographies splitting of the chapter, which doesn't let me fit everything else into it.

❤

25 October

I spent yesterday morning in Nancy Nichols' hillside house in Fremantle Road. Nancy is in her mid – or late? – fifties, grey-haired, and diffident. I came to her through her cousin Polly Gaster, and came to Polly's (tenuous) link with Rose through Victor Gollancz's *Reminiscences of Affection*, in which he mentions *en passant* that Sylvia and Robert Lynd's younger daughter BJ (short for Baby Junior) married a communist called Jack Gaster. And I thought, surely there can only be one communist called Jack Gaster, and that's Polly's Dad. And I was right. And when I wrote to Polly in Maputo and asked her if by any chance she had any correspondence between her grandmother, Sylvia Lynd, and Rose, she said no but her cousin Nancy might have something.

I sat at Nancy's kitchen table and read Sylvia Lynd's unpublished memoir, which is annotated by BJ, Nancy's aunt, Polly's mother. Nancy told me that none of her generation could understand why BJ wanted to spend such an inordinate amount of time on all this stuff of her mother's. And, just as I had felt in Mary Anne O'Donovan's sitting-room, leafing through all her family papers, so I felt pretty strange in Nancy's basement kitchen reading bits and pieces about love affairs between people long dead. Pretty strange – but totally gripped! From the journal I gather Rose and Sylvia were good friends in a literary gossipy sort of way.

BJ was painted at least once if not twice by Mark Gertler, some of whose letters and cards, said Nancy, lie tumbled somewhere in amongst the various bags of family papers in her possession.

Her attitude to this heap of papers from the past is curiously similar to Mary Anne O'Donovan's: 'Oh, all this *stuff* – I don't think I can be bothered to go through it all – sometimes I just want to throw it all away.'

Perhaps I would feel similarly burdened. Or not? No – I'd be completely fascinated. But that's because my mother's parents are a mystery. They're lost in the past; her mother vanished from her life when she was ten, and then my mother herself left home (and her father) when she was fourteen or fifteen. And my dad's father: twenty-five years on the Gold Coast, then sliding into sleeping sickness and dying when Dad was only sixteen. Is it the public aspect of the lives of their parents and grandparents that the O'Donovan and Lynd descendants feel alienated from; or is it their private lives?

Nancy's mother Sigle (pronounced Sheila) worked for the *Daily Worker* and then the *Morning Star* all her life. When the children were small the two families – Nancy's and Polly's – all lived together in a big house crammed with communist lodgers next-door to Granny Lynd in Keats Grove in Hampstead.

><>

3 November

To London yesterday and spent the afternoon in the British Library, reading Rose's anthology *The Minor Pleasures of Life*: a lot of 17th-century material: Milton, Cowley, Burton, Browne and of course Herrick, an old favourite of Rose's, a distant relation of hers and one of the heroes of *They Were Defeated*, where we see him as the large-hearted vicar of Dean Prior, tutor to young Julian Conybeare. The anthology also contains a number of works by Anon, the authorship of one of which – a poem about the 'Delightfull Girles' of Artemis – Rose herself later admitted to. She includes some excerpts from her father's translation of *Herodotus*, and a surprising amount – especially as there are hardly any other American writers – of Walt Whitman. And the peace anthology she put together with Daniel George, *All in a Maze*; how passionately peace was debated then – unlike now, when the bombs we're dropping on Afghanistan are miniaturized, silenced and distanced by the screen of television. If you're not paying a price, how can you imagine what it's like to suffer it? Rose and her generation had paid a price in the Great War. No wonder she was a pacifist in the 1930s.

Then I went on to Bedford Square where I was meeting Jill Nicholls at a Newnham fund-raising party for the new library and the Skilliter Centre for Ottoman Studies which the library is going to house. The party was held in the house of Frances Partridge, who was chatting gaily to people from her armchair in a corner, aged 101. I've no idea why I was invited as I'm not exactly in the rich patron class. Nor is Jill, who's even worse off than me and gets almost no money from the (long-departed) father of her two children. It was a good excuse to see Jill anyway. We chatted to Jean and Richard Gooder (Richard's legs are now so weak – or stiff? – that when he's standing up he has to prop himself against a table edge, or window sill), to Mary Beard who wrote a very intelligent book on the classical scholar Jane Harrison and the whole business of biographical writing, and to nice Jan Marsh who wrote the excellent *Pre-Raphaelite Sisterhood* and a biography of Christina Rossetti that I haven't yet read. She knows Polly Gaster and Nancy Nichols and was in what she called 'a left group' with them when they were all fifteen or sixteen. I thought maybe she meant the Young Communist League, but she told me later she was referring to the London Schools Left Club, which used to meet upstairs in a Soho pub called The Partisan and listen to Left luminaries such as Raphael Samuel, Ralph Miliband, and Raymond Williams. Jan's husband is a professional fund-raiser; he said he was hoping he might be able to help Newnham organise itself more efficiently and move beyond the polite let's-talk-about-women's-scholarship-and-not-mention-money mindset. A friend and contemporary of Jan Marsh's – a professor of ancient history at King's – said she was chair of some rich society that had pots of money to give away to archives and libraries but how, oh how could she get the money to Newnham? Nobody from Newnham would tell her. A S Byatt gave a speech about how important Newnham's library had been to her mother (didn't I read somewhere that her mother suffered terribly from depression, so I guess she experienced her later life as a falling-off from those happy Newnham days?), and how important it had been to her, too. She called it the silent heart of the college. It made me feel I hadn't quite appreciated it while there, having barely set foot in it, preferring the University Library or the English library where at least you could see some men.

Then Jill and I went on to the Serpent's Tail 15th anniversary party just round the corner, in a low dive behind Russell Square. A very different kettle of fish: no sooner had we walked in than a drunken Serpent's Tail author (I recognised her from her picture in the catalogue) fell over on top of me and sent me staggering into the wall; D was knocking back the vodka and soon after our arrival she went off with (went off with? that's what Jill and I thought) a smooth-haired blonde woman from the South Bank. Pete Ayrton as urbane as ever.

I'm beginning to feel desperate to spend a week on my Dorothy L Sayers play (at Sara's suggestion, now entitled, because it's about the birth and therefore as it were genealogy of Lord Peter Wimsey, *De'Ath Bredon*), but can I afford to put Rose aside? I haven't yet finished the 1930s chapter.

>●

6 November

Ivy Compton-Burnett, her hair sculpted as ever like an over-turned chamber pot, appeared as a silent but powerful presence in my dreams of last night.

>●

13 November

In the Boston Tea Party in Bristol, upstairs at a window table looking down on Park Street, waiting to have a cup of tea with Viv French. The story for the Walker anthology for teenaged reluctant readers that Viv commissioned from me – my sinister-tapping-at-the-window ghost story – is apparently due out any day now. Viv is planning to leave Bristol for Edinburgh, as Diana has recently done. I miss Diana and I shall miss Viv too. Viv's got I think two daughters in Edinburgh already, and will be moving up there with her partner and youngest daughter. She told me that once when she was doing a school event someone asked her how many children she had, and she replied 'five', and realised immediately that that wasn't true but felt too embarrassed to correct it. It made me laugh.

I have just spent a couple of hours in Bristol University library's Penguin special collection archives looking at the files on Rose's books: *Crewe Train* (Penguin number 175, published 1938), *Orphan Island*, *Told By An Idiot*, and *The World My Wilderness*. The file on *Dangerous Ages*, her first Penguin (number 76, published 1937) is missing.

When I opened the copy of *The World My Wilderness*, which Hannah the archivist had brought out from the shelves of Penguin first editions that are kept in a special room, I found slipped inside the front cover a strip of paper with Rose's signature on it, snipped off the bottom of a letter I had already seen in the cardboard folder. For a moment I entertained a brief fantasy about taking it. Like Roland Michell in the London Library in A S Byatt's *Possession*, I was seized by a 'strange and uncharacteristic impulse'. Do all biographers become possessed by the urge to own something, to have a little bit of their subject just for themselves, I wonder? Not that Rose's signature on a scrap of paper is of any value or indeed particular interest – and anyway I already own some of her signed books – but the pointlessness of such a theft is not what's relevant. Perhaps it's the act of taking, of exerting physical mastery over a relic of the subject, that carries the emotional freight, rather than what it is that you take. (Although what Roland Michell finds and takes, or rather steals, is far from insignificant.)

Anyway when the archivist re-emerged with the other books I showed her the autographed scrap. Well apparently that was what Allen Lane did with books that hadn't been signed by the author: he snipped their autograph from elsewhere and slid it between the first few pages. For one of Virginia Woolf's books he cut her signature from a cheque she'd signed (why was Virginia Woolf sending a cheque to Allen Lane I wonder?). Later, when I went through to Hannah's office to ask if she would photocopy something for me, I saw that the readers' desk where I had been sitting was displayed on a CCTV screen in a corner of the room. What if I had pinched the autograph, and Hannah had watched me doing it? The horrible shameful idea made me break out in a sweat.

In the correspondence file for *The World My Wilderness* I read about allegations of libel, brought by the director of the 'dubious' Japanese company whose building Barbary passes on one of her walks through the streets of the City of London. This was after Rose's death, and Penguin agreed to gum an apology into the remaining books. In the other files I found various letters from Rose complaining about the 'superlatives' of the biographical blurbs, which I took as examples of what I've become familiar with: an irritating, oh, why should anyone be interested in little me? Then when I looked at the actual file copies, I saw at once why Rose had objected: brilliant this and brilliantly witty that ... On and on, completely over the top. Her objections now strike me as entirely reasonable.

A lovely two hours. Whereas yesterday, yesterday – I think I always find Mondays difficult because the weekends are so filled with domestic responsibilities that it takes me time to get back into intellectual work on a Monday. But then I should feel ... pleased at the prospect of five days work ahead. But my 1930s chapter is a huge shapeless lump, 15,000 words long, and it seems like such an effort to hammer and cut it into shape. And I've gone on so much about the biographies and *They Were Defeated* and not really about her life, and sometimes I think – yesterday I thought – who will want to read this? Where is Rose's life?

16 November

Spent today and yesterday on *De'Ath Bredon*. What a change to work on something that you know isn't going to be very long. It feels light and pleasurable and – easy, I suppose. There are still problems with Sayers's beloved John Cournos and Bill White, the father of her baby, being whisked on and then whisked off again before you've barely had time to make their acquaintance. I remember the same problem arose with my first ever play – my first ever play! as if I'm some kind of Alan Ayckbourn or Simon Gray, whereas the truth is *Thin Woman* was only my second ever play. I wrote my first ever play, title forgotten, in my first year at Cambridge and it was directed by Stephen Poliakoff, in King's College cellars, when he was still an undergraduate and before he was even famous at all. It required two actors, one to play a dreaming youth, and the other, played by Jill Nicholls, to be all the people that he dreams of. She had to dash on and off at top speed and change out of one costume and into another with only a minute or so between scenes. All the boy had to do was lie there and dream. No – there must have been dialogue! Surely! Who played him? I think it was that very tall fair-haired boy from Corpus who was sweet on Jane Rogers. I heard of him years later in some terribly prestigious diplomatic post in Paris. Jill was heroic with the costume changes, one of which was a clingy, drooping Arthurian Lady-type outfit. I had been reading Malory.

I heard today from Barbara Reynolds or rather via her from someone called Christopher who she'd passed it on to, who may or may not be (but probably is) the author of the *Lord Peter Wimsey Companion*, that the two lines Harriet Vane quotes in *Gaudy Night*:

> *You not alone, when you are alone,*
> *Oh God, from you that I could private be!*

come from Michael Drayton, early 17th century, his *Idea in Sixty-Three Sonnets*, which sounds more like a work by HD or Ezra Pound than by someone who died the same year as John Donne. Drayton sounds familiar to me Rose-wise. Does she use him in an epigraph? Or is he in *Minor Pleasures*? I can't remember. Is 'Roger Rampole's Cheaping', a fake 'Anon' Rose-authored epigraph to *I Would be Private*, a pastiche of Drayton? 'Press me not, throng me not, by your leave I would be private ...' But prose not poetry. Drayton wrote a clutch of poems about the Battle of Agincourt one of which starts with the famous 'Fayre stood the wind for France ...' How does it go on? I'd better look it up: '... When we our sails advance,/ Nor now to prove our chance,/ Longer will tarry.'

When I got home on Monday I found a message on the answer machine from Hannah, the archivist in the University Library. Had I by mistake taken one of the Rose Macaulay files, as she could find only three instead of four. What?? I immediately felt guilty as accused, as if thought had nightmarishly transmuted into deed, and scrap of autograph, monstrously, into bulging file. I knew I hadn't – I mean you can't take a file by mistake. But I felt I had to check amongst my notebooks just in case – just in case of what? That I had actually taken it? I rang her to say I definitely hadn't got it, but didn't say that obviously she must have put it back in the wrong place herself. Which, as it turned out, she had – but didn't discover until the next morning, when she rang and apologised.

><>

20 November

After my teaching yesterday one of the lecturers in the English department, the nice Danish one called Ad, said to me, 'Oh, didn't I hear you had got some terribly prestigious prize for your book – British Academy or something?' What a pleasing rumour to have in circulation. But I had to tell him no.

><>

22 November

Dreamed last night that I was just starting as an undergraduate at York University, which admitted only girls. I wonder at what age one starts dreaming of a younger self, rather than just of a self, or dream-self; or whether your dream-self becomes increasingly a younger self as you get older? In the dream I didn't question what age I was; it was when I woke up this morning that I thought: how could I possibly be an undergraduate? I'm much too old.

><

29 November

The war/1940s chapter is coming on quite fast, tho I had a bit of a crisis yesterday afternoon reading some of Constance's biography and thinking 'am I just rewriting Constance and Jane Emery? What's the point of writing this book?' Get thee behind me.

I'm loving *They Went to Portugal*. So quirky and racy and flowing. I'm at last beginning to understand why Rose Macaulay saw herself as not primarily a fiction writer. But perhaps she had to write novels for twenty years in order to 'be a writer' in her own eyes. She had to create those credentials for herself first. Perhaps.

Jill had a fiftieth birthday party on Saturday night. Fifty! The last birthday party of hers I remember was in Cambridge, in Christchurch Street, when she was twenty-two. And Judy Kimble was still alive. I can't remember who came to it. I was her only Cambridge friend there on Saturday, but I wasn't her oldest friend – that was tiny Claire Lawton, with whom Jill was at school, accompanied by her extremely large husband Patrick Wright. At first sight Claire, a consultant psychiatrist, looks the very picture of a prim, respectable doctor, and then you notice her scarlet stiletto-heeled pointy-toed snakeskin shoes. She is certainly forthright and combative in her opinions. I like her very much. And I like Patrick, who told us an astonishing story about how, some months – into researching for his history of the tank – *Tank*, his book's called – he realised there was another Patrick Wright, who must be some high-up person in defence; and it was because of the existence of this other Patrick Wright that he, this Patrick Wright, was getting clearance from the Pentagon to go and look round Fort Knox for three days, and from the Israeli high command to interview one of their generals. But then one of the Israelis became suspicious ...

Jill was putting on public display for the first time her new boyfriend Dave Veltmann. He's an artist – a painter – who earns a living as a builder. He puts in a lot of basement swimming pools for the Hassids up the hill. He struck me as very genial, intelligent, kind and altogether highly suitable. In fact he and Jill are not dissimilar physically: short, slightly built, with mobile, expressive faces. I think they make a good – and handsome – pair. I hope she'll keep him.

12 December

I have reached the end of the 'In Ruins' chapter this morning, with Rose just clambering out of the ruins of the 1940s. Marjorie Grant Cook has insistently reappeared. I quote her wonderful letter to Jonathan Cape in 1946 going on about her detestable and dreadful book, and how her next one is a melodrama, and she can promise that no character in it is pregnant or pious. But what was her next one? Why is she so elusive?

I have just googled Marjorie GC. Should have thought of that before! It took me straight to the *Times Literary Supplement* centenary archive, which begins: ' ... among the most prolific of contributors to the *Times Literary Supplement* in the 20s and 30s was Marjorie Grant Cook ... reviewed more than 1200 books ...' One or two reviews a week, every week: no wonder she didn't have much time for writing her own books! She wouldn't of course have been known as a *Times Literary Supplement* reviewer as all reviews were unsigned. How much did she get paid, I wonder? Apparently she championed Willa Cather. And later, *The Hobbit.*

13 December

Robert Lynd's selected essays, *Galway of the Races*, came this week via inter-library loan from the James Hardiman library in Galway. It has a good introduction by Sean McMahon. Polly Gaster is mentioned by name. It's so strange to read about the mother and grandparents of someone you know. Sylvia's mother had an affair with Nevinson, editor of the *Times*, and left her husband for him; Sylvia had an 'unconsummated', according to McMahon, love affair with someone, and was in bed for six months with a broken heart, or depression. Hmm … Was it depression? Nancy told me Sylvia had a string of miscarriages, so presumably she might have been in bed recovering from them or trying to save the pregnancies – she was rhesus negative, so it was rather remarkable that she managed to successfully give birth to a second baby.

Robert Lynd was more central a literary figure in the 20s and 30s, and especially in Irish London, than I had realised, with a weekly column in the *New Statesman* for years and years. But he fell into silence. Depressed, too?

Our eldest child came home from university yesterday for the Christmas holidays. 'Hey, Mum,' he said last night, 'Look at this. Your Constance Babington Smith makes an appearance in Thomas Pynchon's *Gravity's Rainbow.*' And there she is, on page 726, almost at the end of the book: '… the City will always be changing, new tire-treads in the dust, new cigarette wrappers in the garbage … engineering changes to the Rocket create new routes of supply, new living arrangements, reflected in traffic densities as viewed from this unusual height – there are indeed tables of Functions to get from such City-changes to Rocket-modifications: no more than an extension, really, of the techniques by which Constance Babington Smith and her colleagues at RAF Medmenham discovered the Rocket back in 1943 in recco photographs of Peenemünde.'

><

19 December

The Durham University librarian has copied for me and sent a series of letters that Rose wrote to William Plomer, whose memoirs I read way back three and a half years ago when I was just embarking on the Rose journey. Most of them are post-*The Towers of Trebizond*, and they talk much of *Towers* and the church; the tone is considerably less sanctimonious than in the letters to dreary old Father Hamilton Johnson, edited by Constance. Rose describes herself to Plomer as Anglo-agnostic, and praises the broadness of the C of E for allowing so much difference within it. She expresses the joy of belonging without conforming.

At Dad's birthday lunch on the 14th I was sitting next to Mum and she suddenly, to my surprise, started talking about her past: her abandoning mother, her shell-shocked father and her sister Joan, eighteen months younger than her, who killed herself (it was thought) in her early twenties by jumping off a cliff into the sea. Mum was working as a land-girl in Watchet when the police turned up to tell her.

✺

24 December

Last night at about 11.30 I went to pick up our eldest child from the Chelvey party – the annual party hosted together by the two families that live, one in the upper storey and the other below, in the ancient thick-walled house – and parked, cunningly I thought, outside the church, as I didn't want to have to go up the long winding drive and park somewhere in the dark on the grass amongst the trees. I had never before taken the path to the house through the churchyard, but earlier in the evening when I'd been at the party myself I had noticed a number of people parking outside the churchyard and walking through. So I opened the metal lych-gate, and stepped straight into a deep inky darkness underneath the yews. To my right the dark bulk of the church loomed, enclosing, it seemed to me, a large area of even darker darkness. As I looked at it, it seemed to increase in size. Silence all around. Ahead of me, in the direction of the house, I began to see, illuminated by the windows beyond, coils of smoke or mist creeping and curling over the tops of the gravestones. I tripped, and fell over a gravestone, and suddenly some lights on the church flashed on and I saw I was way off the path, and I thought, 'what am I doing here, stumbling around a graveyard on my own in the middle of the night?'

I could feel little flutters of fear in my stomach, but I forced myself to walk slowly towards the far gate, past a smoking stump which was all that was left of a flaming torch set up earlier in the evening to light the path. I felt as if I was crammed full of fear and excitation, and words tumbled out of my mouth as soon as I got into the house. It so happened that the first two people I saw were Kate and Jacqui, joint hosts of the party. Surely these are two of the most sensible women of my acquaintance, one an artist and arts commissioner, the other a secondary school teacher, both with families, husbands, households that they appear to run with enviable calmness and efficiency. I would never have dreamt that either of them harboured fears of the supernatural, but after I had spilled out my own terror, Jacqui immediately told me that on no account would she ever take a short-cut through the graveyard at night, and had never done so in the twenty years she'd lived there. Kate took up the baton with a long riff on the unease she feels about the common grave of three babies beneath a gravestone carved with 'tempus fugit', which lies just inside the churchyard gate, a stone's throw from her back door.

Which was the more surprising? That these two successful, practical women should feel so vulnerable to hauntings, or that they should carry on living in such a ghost-thick place?

Later I thought about the two ghost stories that Rose wrote: the wine-loving, sun-seeking life-affirming pre-World War One ghost of 'The Empty Berth' followed, forty years later, by the ghost of the Emperor Tiberius in 'Whitewash'. 'Are we to be deprived of all the monsters of the past?' asks the scarlet burnous-wearing aunt – an Aunt Dot-like figure (Macaulay 1952, 70). In both stories the ghosts are educators, or revealers; in 'Whitewash' the narrator (an 'I' narrator and, like Laurie for most of *Towers*, ambiguously gendered) experiences the true Tiberius, who laughs as he pushes his terrified victims into the jaws of a great white shark. It's a powerful story. I suppose you could say that 'Miss Anstruther's Letters' is also a sort of ghost story, in that Miss Anstruther herself is presented as a drifting ghost. No – I think ghosts are the dead returned – for one reason or another – to the land of the living. Miss Anstruther is alive. She feels herself to be insubstantial like a ghost, unconnected to the living world, but she isn't one. Nor is her lover – he's dead and gone and irrecoverable.

Chapter Eleven: January–May 2002

Home/London/Cambridge/Home)

1 January

A cold clear frosty day. In the shade of the yew and the orchard hedge the grass was rimed with hoar all day. Last year started badly in a number of ways; but then I was given the Arts Council Award at the end of March which more than made up for residual feelings of failure that had been rekindled at the new year. The Award has made such a difference; it has made me feel confident even through the difficult writing patches.

Now I've got almost no money left after Christmas, but fortunately I've got some teaching lined up for the next eight weeks. And the fee for my Radio 4 abridgement of *The Towers of Trebizond* is due – although they're allowing only a week's worth, five programmes, so I won't get much more than £500 altogether. Still, better than a slap in the face with a wet fish, as they say. As most things are. Sara Davies, producing, has advised cutting the Charles/David/plagiarism strand, all those young men and their Turkey books, which is a pity, but with only 10,000 or so words allowed in total for the abridgement, there's really only space for the basic journeying, Vere's death and Laurie's exile from the shimmering towers. But Sara's agreed that we'll try hard to include Mr Yorum.

>–●

8 January

Our middle child's sixteenth birthday. I've been trying to remember my own sixteenth birthday, but can't even recall where I was. Did we still live in Edinburgh, or had Mum and Dad moved to Zagreb? They were in Zagreb when I was seventeen, after my A Levels – but sixteen? It was a pretty grim time for me. I'd been at Cheltenham for a year and hated it and was about to go back for another year. In fact I do now remember suffering my usual beginning-of-term illness, lying in bed with a sore throat in Fauconberg – which was the upper sixth house, so I must have been just sixteen. I think HB is happier than I was at that age – well, I'm sure she is – and so she should be! She's not at some ghastly boarding school for a start. Anne McIvor, one of the two friends I made at Cheltenham and who arrived, like me, for the sixth form, loathed the place so much she got her father to remove her after that first year. Skinny blonde Anne was my partner in crime when we sneaked off out of school to attend Brian Jones's funeral, and were picked up by two *News of the World* journalists who offered us a lift back to 'town', by which they meant London and we, embarrassingly, understood Cheltenham, where we had left our tell-tale green uniform bundled in newspaper in the hedge behind the public lavatories in the park. I seem to remember Anne was forbidden by her father to have anything to do with her two older half-brothers for fear of some undefined corrupting influence; when I was staying with her in the holidays we used to meet them in secret at a bar in a hotel off Hyde Park.

Rose Macaulay at sixteen had been back in England for three years after her wild barelegged childhood by the sea in Varazze; now she was dressed in cheap brown corduroy and button boots and attended Oxford High School with her sisters Margaret and Jean where they were trained in 'true religion, good manners and sound learning'. Rose found it all 'pretty dim', but I'm sure it was nowhere near as bad as Cheltenham, and anyway they went back to Italy for winter holidays, and the siblings still had each other. Rose at about sixteen poses for a girl-and-dog photo: it's the late 1890s and she's still muffled up in tight-waisted full-sleeved Victorian gear with her long hair tied back with ribbons. She has an arm around the dog, a mongrely-looking terrier type. (Tom? No, I think he came later.) It's standing on its hind legs with its front paws in her lap, and looks straight at the camera, whereas she is obliquely dreaming.

When I came back from East Africa at eleven I swapped shorts, T-shirts, and tackies, for hairy tweed skirts, viyella blouses (with strangling tie), and leather lace-ups.

><>

14 January

Have been looking once more at *Letters* and *Last Letters to a Friend*. Rose's re-entry to the church was neither a *volte-face* nor was it total submersion/submission. She's very careful to hang on to the outsider role even once she's inside. Her attitude is interrogative and disputatious while simultaneously she enjoys the peace and security that being 'in' provides – lucky her, you might say. Rose writes to Hamilton Johnson about her new-found friend Constance Babington Smith. She 'began by making smart hats, then fell in love with planes, and once designed a hat made like a bomber, which she wore at an aeronautic garden party' (Macaulay 1963, 258). I wish I could find a photo of lovely pretty Constance in her bomber hat.

22 January

A cup of Turkish tea from Rize is steaming by my right hand. I'm hoping that it will inspire me to write about *Towers* with imagination and with insight. I spent the whole of yesterday marking-up a copy of *Towers* for a first draft of the Radio 4 abridgement. God what a laborious way of doing it! It would be even more laborious if I were obliged to actually type up the draft. I flatly refused to do so; at my typing speed I'd end up being paid about 2p an hour for the abridgement. Some poor minion at the BBC is having to do it. Wouldn't it be quicker for them to scan the whole text into a computer? Maybe not.

On Saturday a copy of the new *Arvon Journal* arrived, with my short piece on Trebizond, and an excellent largish reproduction of one of the photos Mon took, from the *meydan*, of the *Yeşilyurt Otel*, which we'd had to take surreptitiously, pretending we were photographing some buses, in case anyone – *Yeşilyurt* management or the creepy 'tourist police' – thought we were gathering evidence of the hotel's current use as a brothel. The front cover shows a small picture of me gazing at some rocks in the Black Sea.

24 January

I have been writing up an exchange in the *Times Literary Supplement*: in 1955 Rose had a poem called 'Dirge for Trebizond' published in its pages and was duly taken to task by the Press Attaché at the Turkish Embassy, Mr Pamir, for referring in the poem to Turks as 'barbarians'. She wriggled out of it by saying she was speaking as Byzantines (rather than Rose Macaulay) spoke about Turks, and anyway Greeks used to refer to all non-Greeks as barbarians. Pedantry, I'd say – it's an aspect of Rose's character I really don't like. But maybe she felt uncomfortable about it all, because she sort of made up for it in *Towers* by giving nice, sympathetic, put-upon Dr Halide some of the Attaché's arguments against Western feelings of superiority.

><

2 February

Clevedon sea front. A brown muddy sea, higher than usual, running fast. Steep Holm Island crouches clear on the horizon.

Yesterday I sent off what I've written of Chapter 12 to Michèle and Jenny. And at once fell to thinking how dull it is, much too much about the books, too ploddingly literary. Perhaps I haven't put enough (or any?) of *my* Trebizond into the chapter? Perhaps I should – it might liven it up. I think I've been thinking, unconsciously: 'I've written that up, it's been broadcast, so that's it, I can't re-use it.' But of course I can. And it might make a welcome break for the reader from whether I think *The World my Wilderness* works as a novel or not, or whether or not I consider Laurie's feelings re the Church to be Rose's own.

Last night I watched a documentary about US army atrocities against civilians in South Korea. Most of what I know about the Korean war comes from MASH – and I often think of the MASH film I saw, unexpectedly, on the telly one night twenty or so years ago. I thought it was going to be a comedy but suddenly it was about Hawk-Eye having a nervous breakdown, as a result of him travelling in a truck, or on a coach, with some civilians and nearly driving into an ambush. A peasant woman was sitting on the back seat with a chicken that kept squawking, and in the end Hawk-Eye turned to her and told her to shut it up if they didn't all want to be caught and killed – and she wrung its neck. Only it wasn't a chicken, it was her baby. That scene has haunted me ever since. Last night one of the interviewees, one of the Korean peasants who had survived this particular US massacre, told how all the villagers had been hiding from the American soldiers in a tunnel or cave. A baby was crying, and the Americans were shooting into the tunnel aiming at where they could hear the cries coming from. To shut it up and save everyone else from being shot the father of the baby held it face down in a dirty puddle on the ground until it drowned. Is this particular to the Korean war? Or had the MASH film screenwriter known the story of the US atrocity and drew on it for the film? Or is people having to sacrifice their babies to save the community a common occurrence in wars where a peasant/civilian population is terrorised by men with guns?

><>

7 February

Writers' group meeting with Jenny and Michèle on Monday. Helpful, but I think they thought my chapter was more finished than it is, and so they were more critical than I would have liked them to be. Then I drank too much wine and felt ill as a result. Later we went with Michèle to an Amnesty benefit in the Players Theatre in Villiers Street, where she read a couple of pages of her very funny story about a woman who stalks a celebrity chef. Some of the other writers read for what felt like hours.

British Library on Tuesday. I sat in the top Humanities reading room, into which at least a few rays of natural light penetrate, and read Margaret Macaulay's novel, *The Sentence Absolute*, which is set in the valley outside Aberystwyth where the Macaulay family lived in the early 1900s and is peopled with high-minded girls and weak-willed chaps. But the hero turns out OK in the end, and the girl learns tolerance and forgiveness. I wonder if it's a re-working of the Macaulay/ Brooke connection: Tony Venning (Dick Brooke) is flawed, but not so flawed that he succumbs, as Dick Brooke did, to alcoholism, and he marries Gwen (Margaret) in the end. (Whereas Dick Brooke was dead at twenty-six.) It's certainly not as despairingly dark as Rose's 'Welsh' novel *The Valley Captives*.

11. The photograph of Rose Macaulay in her flat in the 1950s, now on
    display at the London Library.

Then I walked to the London Library, where, in a well-lit corner of
the reading room on the first floor Rose is commemorated with a
comfortable red leather armchair beneath a framed photograph
of her working in her flat in the 1950s. A plaque says, 'This corner of
the Reading Room has been furnished in Rose Macaulay's memory
by her friends'. In the photo Rose is sitting on her floral-covered sofa
typing away with her typewriter on her lap and pieces of paper and
open books scattered on a low table at her knee and balanced on the
sofa's fat arm. Three pictures hang on the wall behind her: the middle
one shows two sailing boats safe within harbour walls, with the boats
themselves enclosing two tiny tug boats. They all look safe from the
sea and from a fierce surf-surrounded black rock top left. One of
the other pictures looks rather like a Gwen John: it shows an empty
armchair and a little table by a window looking out over a park; the
third is a painting of trees, a distant mountain, and you can just make

out a funny-looking building – I think this might be Denton Welch's *The Coffin-House*, but I'm not sure. Rose wears a dark jacket over a spotted shirt with a big fanned bow at the neck. A spotted handkerchief peeps out of a breast pocket. At some point she asked the London Library that her early novels – *Abbots Verney*, *The Furnace*, *The Secret River*, *The Valley Captives* and *Views and Vagabonds* – be removed from the shelves and thrown away. What librarian would accede to such a request? They are locked in a safe in the Librarians' Room – her other books are on the open shelves.

On Tuesday evening I accompanied Michèle to a jolly launch party at Lennie Goodings' house for Sarah Waters' *Fingersmith*. All Sarah's relations from Wales were there, along with a number of very young and sweet-looking women and Jane from Silver Moon bookshop whom I hadn't seen in years. Yesterday morning I visited the Lansdowne Club and its subterranean art-deco swimming pool, where Rose was towed up and down on a lilo by Rosamond Lehmann, and where she leapt, wearing a massive swimming hat like an ancient martial casque, from the top board, or hurled herself down the wooden chute to plunge into the water like a knife. Neither high board nor wooden chute remain. Probably considered too dangerous. Rosamond Lehmann recounts how amazed she was when she discovered that Rose, for all her obsessive swimming everywhere she possibly could, actually couldn't swim terribly well at all. I was amazed too. The Lansdowne Club is fearfully posh. I would've liked a swim myself but didn't have a costume and anyway the invitation wasn't forthcoming.

5 March

On Friday I parcelled up Draft One, chapters 1-13, and sent it to Judith Murray. The previous ten days had been non-stop: it takes such a long time just to read, let alone think of re-writing, and I didn't want to send it off in too rough a state. If you do send it rough, people always concentrate on the weak sentences, which you know are weak anyway, and they don't read for the broader picture. So I was trying to get rid of those weak sentences. Anyway, off it went. And yesterday I went to

Oxford and spent the day in the Bodleian – I am now a 'Bodleian reader' it says on my card – reading the Rose/Gilbert Murray correspondence on microfilm: chatty, engaged with the world, affectionate (increasingly, on his side). He remained 'Dear Professor Murray' until into the 1950s, when, after twenty years of friendship, he became 'dear Gilbert'.

6 March

Lees-Milne's diaries are sharp and funny. He's hilarious on the way that Ivy Compton-Burnett and Margaret Jourdain used to stuff food into their mouths, and the way Ivy used to shout down anyone who said something she disagreed with. His affection for them also comes over. He's a very good diarist, which perhaps is missed by people who dismiss him as a snob. Well, he *is* a snob – but also brilliantly observant.

7 March

Benefit anthologies: Rose contributed to at least two, if not more, during the First World War. One was for the Belgians, one for the Red Cross. Rupert Brooke was published (via Eddie Marsh) in the Red Cross one. Then later there was Rose's badly timed – 1939 – Peace Anthology. I wonder when the concept started, of writers doing their bit by contributing to books? I can't believe they did it during the Crimean war, or the Boer war. Perhaps the First World War was the start. It's nice to think that that is a small link between Rose and myself – with *Colours of a New Day: Writing for South Africa*. Which reminds me of the potential plagiarism scandal Stephen Hayward and I were caught up in, when we were informed by Random House USA that one of our contributors had copied almost word for word a story – I think maybe it was an excerpt from a novel, I can't remember – by one of their writers. We'd been particularly impressed by our black South African contributor writing from the point of view of a white liberal Jewish South African; rather less impressed when we discovered that the original piece was indeed authored by a white liberal Jewish South African. We managed to dissuade Random House from demanding that we pulp the whole print run. Our contributor refused to admit the plagiarism but became very high-handed with us. Do plagiarists think they won't be found out? Do they think they're too clever to be found out? I think that the act of deception is based on an assumption of superiority: if someone *can* be deceived, then they *deserve* to be deceived because they're stupid. But what did this bloke think the original author would do when he found out? David in *Towers* thinks, mistakenly, that his theft will go undetected now that Charles has been eaten by a shark. In our case, in an anthology of work which includes a number of pieces by South African writers in exile, the theft was positively flaunted. Stephen and I were livid.

The child I was leading on Boogie this afternoon at Riding for the Disabled, a six- or seven-year-old with severe attention deficit problems and as a result bloody annoying at times, was allowed, because his mum was following us in her car, to stay on Boogie's back while I led him along the lane back to his field after the session. As we came around the curve of the corner and saw sheep and cows grazing in the fields that stretch downhill on either side of the lane, and the twigs of the still bare hedges gleaming in the afternoon sunshine, the little boy said, 'This is a big adventure.' My heart went out to him.

March 12: Paddington

Have just been in Broadcasting House recording a piece on Rose for *Open Book*, with an odd but charming dog-collared woman vicar called Terrence somebody. As usual I was stomach-churningly nervous beforehand – it's absurd, as it's not as if I have anything to lose, such as a job – but I think it went fine. I came up yesterday and stayed with Mum and Dad and asked them this morning if I could talk to both of them about their lives and record it. I had been nervous of asking – sometimes I feel I'm not cut out to be a biographer – and Mum hmmed and hah-ed – but I think they will, and this would be my chance to get on with seeking my lost maternal grandmother.

Must write to Nigel Nicolson re Rose and ask if I can interview him. Why do I not think of these things earlier?

18 March

Barton Road, Cambridge, staying again with Sheila Stern. In her bedroom Sheila has two marvellous photos of her husband Peter the historian, out with the Cambridgeshire hunt. In one he's astride his large horse facing the camera, top hatted, grinning. Apparently the horse was shared with another don. There were only three of them from the university in the hunt; the third was an enormous man from Corpus Christi. The other photo is taken from the rear; the horse's rounded rump looms huge in the centre, above it Peter crouches enthusiastically forwards over its neck, and they're galloping flat out away from us over a bare ploughed field, his coat-tails flapping.

In 1939 Peter was eighteen. He fled Prague – his mother killed herself after the Nazis seized their house – and walked across Europe to the English Channel. When he reached England he was billeted with a Welsh couple on Barry Island and spoke English thereafter with a marked Welsh-Czech accent. Later, after a year at St John's College, Cambridge, he joined one of the two Czech squadrons of the RAF as a rear gunner. Tessa had told me all of this before. This evening as we drank our martinis Sheila told me of Peter's wartime adventures: he was shot down over the sea a hundred miles west of Cornwall, but was rescued by a passing trawler sailed by a group of SOE pretending to be fishermen. It sounds absurdly like *The Towers of Trebizond*, in which Albanians pretend to be Greek fishermen, and British physicists masquerade as yachtsmen. Peter's best friend, the front gunner, didn't survive. The SOE took Peter to Cornwall, where he survived an aerial attack on the Red Cross ambulance that was transporting him to a military hospital, and then a bombing raid on the hospital itself in which sixteen nurses were killed. The only permanent damage he incurred was to his spine and the loss of half his left hand.

I realized when I re-read *Towers* last year that I could have learnt about martinis from Rose herself, had I been paying attention. When Laurie returns to London from Trebizond she is made neurotic and unhappy when she finds a massive pile of unpaid bills and demands from the taxman. 'Presently I had a martini to pull myself together,' she says. I know exactly what she means now. Then she abandons the bills to go and ring her lover. And then meditates on the dilemma of love, and adultery.

I turned up at the Wren Library this morning just as it was opening. 'Oh, you again,' said the man with wild hair and a beard. Later, when he came on duty at the readers' desk: 'Haven't you read all this before?' suspiciously. 'I'm sure you have.' And he's right. Some of it, tho not all, I have read before, but as I explained to him, it's different reading it again, now that I know more and so have a different context for my reading.

I thought Byron had a club foot. Today I noticed that his marble feet appear perfectly-formed, and elegantly shod, too.

Walked along the Backs this morning in mild March weather and along the Trinity footpath past thick clusters of crocuses and ranks of shining daffodils. When I came out at 5 pm it was into driving rain and bitter wind and I felt cold and alone.

Once again Mary Anne O'Donovan was very welcoming. I discovered that Rose, her godmother, left her the boat picture that hangs above the sofa in the photo in the London Library. Mary Anne has it in her consulting-room, hanging where her patients can look at it when they lie on the couch. It's ideal for a consulting-room, she says: boats, baby boats, encircling sea, safe harbour walls – and it's lovely colours too, all dark greens and blues. I can imagine how it soothes her patients. Rose left Mary Anne another painting, which she couldn't lay her hands on tonight (not *The Coffin-House* – I think Rose gave that to Mary Anne's mother Muriel, but she was creeped out by it and got rid of it), and her other godmother Marjorie Grant Cook (perhaps she was her sister Jane's godmother) left her a pastel of 'Miss Siddall' by Dante Gabriel Rossetti, according to the label on the back. Apparently Marjorie Grant Cook always said it was 'school of DGR'. Certainly it looks very Rossetti-ish – head of woman looking down, her pale face and neck framed by thick curtains of red hair. The model actually looks not unlike Marjorie Grant Cook herself in another of Mary Anne's pictures: a pencil portrait signed 'Gill'. Mary Anne thinks that it's by one of Gill's sisters, rather than by Eric Gill himself. Dated 1924, Marjorie looks elegant, classical, Bloomsburyish. Is it weird, or is it not weird, that Mary Anne's and Jane's godmothers were/had at some point been their grandfather's mistresses? (Granted I'm using Marjorie Grant Cook's novel *Latchkey Ladies* as evidence for her and Gerald, which wouldn't stand up in court, that's for sure.) I come down on the side of weird.

Mary Anne inherited from Gerald (who was also her godfather) a small portable wooden lectern that she thinks must have come from Loughrea – two wings fold out from the central panel, the whole is decorated with sun, moon, ourobouros, a backward swastika that I know has some Celtic meaning but I can't remember it, feathery bits, an angel ... Celtic revival, in other words ... And on the outside of the panels, when the doors are closed, a deep-carved Celtic cross. Was this given to Gerald when he left Loughrea? Or had he had it made for himself, and been using it in the parish for some time before he left?

Mary Anne told me that Gerald had used to enjoy going to parties and deliberately leaving his hat behind in the hallway – his hat with GO'D inscribed within. Dermod, said Mary Anne of her father, was bitter against his own father because he thought he gave him the wrong advice. But Dermod's letters to his father Gerald in the 1930s are incredibly loving. Gerald's letters to Beryl are loving, too. 'My own darling,' he says. Mary Anne is a generous woman. She said to me: Write what you like. Don't worry about what anyone in the family thinks.

><>

21 March

As Sheila Stern gives much of her time to a veritable flock of lame ducks, I thought that a stay of two nights was enough of a demand from me, and moved to Newnham. Now they charge £20 a night. God, the corridors here. My room is in Peile – it seems like a mile from the Porters' Lodge. No wonder I was never friends with anyone in Peile. I met a lost Dutchwoman dragging her suitcase down the corridor in Clough and directed her ever onwards.

The bed is at right angles to the outside wall, halfway along; its foot juts out into the middle of the room. I dreamt that I was lying there in the bed, and that the walls in front of me and to either side were covered with clothes hanging from hangers, like life-size puppets, and that a wind arose and their teeth started chattering and their limbs jerking, the material of their clothes billowing, their heads lolling and rolling, all high up on the walls around me. I awoke with a racing heart, not daring to move.

><•>

22 March

I'm sitting next to a stove outside the Eagle, drinking a pint of Abbot Ale and reading a new Virago edition of Dodie Smith's *I Capture the Castle*, which Lennie gave me the other day. I started it last night – before my nightmares of lolling-headed puppets on the walls of the room – and laughed aloud over the scene of Rose wearing the fur coat left to her and her sister Cassandra by their great-aunt, and being mistaken for an escaped bear. Later, when Cassandra looks at her sister in a pink muslin frock and ancient crinoline, she thinks of 'Go, lovely Rose' by Edmund Waller:

>'How small a part of time they share
>That are so wondrous sweet and fair!'

Janet Adam Smith entitled her obituary of Rose Macaulay in the *New Statesman* 'Go, happy Rose', from Robert Herrick's song, 'To the Rose'. She writes about Rose's happiness at being so engaged with life, living life to the full in her idiosyncratic and independent way. And ends by suggesting that Rose was very seventeenth-century in her zest and wit and intellectual curiosity, and her unshockability and religious temper.

><•>

26 March

On Friday and Saturday nights all my dreams were filled with turning over pages and pages and pages of letters to and from Rose Macaulay. As if I hadn't done enough of that in real life last week. I am trying now to write the epilogue: the whole complicated story around Constance's Big Plan to publish Rose's letters to Father Hamilton Johnson, in the teeth of Rose's request that all correspondence be destroyed.

><•>

27 March

Another panic-inducing dream last night: that the ghost of Constance Babington Smith had entered my body and was convulsing and upheaving it. When I woke my head was filled with the images of those chattering flapping life-size puppets hanging on the walls of the room that I saw in my dream in Newnham.

Received a cool letter from Nigel Nicolson saying don't bother to come and talk to me, I barely knew the woman. A very different tone from Francis King's courteous letter declining to meet me. But Francis King liked Rose, and I suspect Nicolson didn't. Which reminds me (thinking of Francis King): I must write to nice Gerard Irvine and ask him if he knows what happened to Rose's Denton Welch painting.

I've just checked in *Last Letters*: as I thought, Rose records going to Nigel Nicolson's wedding in 1953, which she refers to as 'the wedding of a friend'. 'But what an *odd* service the marriage service in some ways is!' she writes.

5 April

I've been working on the Epilogue all week: 'Letters', it's called. Perhaps a Prologue called 'Diaries', in which I'd discuss Grace's and her brother Edward's diaries. Then if I put all the ancestor stuff in the introduction, I could start Chapter One with Rose's birth, and move fairly swiftly on to Varazze. Our eldest child asked: why don't you write a novel about biography and possession featuring Constance Babington Smith, or her ghost?

If the epilogue was illustrated, with pictures incorporated into the text, we could have Constance pretty and smiling in her pearl necklace as on the flap of her Rose book – or, better, if I could find such a photo, in her aeronautical garden party bomber hat; Rose looking like a Russian spy as she appeared in the photo in the *Daily Mail* that accompanied one of their articles about the letters, headlined 'Did this priest betray this woman?'; and middle-England frumpy retired nurse Jean. The three women involved in the story of the letters. This kind of playing around with words and images is such fun, but my god the writing is a wrestling, and having wrestled with it for days I now wonder

Did this priest betray this woman?

ROSE MACAULAY

CLOSE friends of Dame Rose Macaulay are horrified at the news that her very intimate letters to a high Anglican priest who had been her confessor are shortly to be published in book form.

They know it is the last thing this exceptionally dignified, fastidious, and reticent woman would have wished, but they have been powerless to stop publication.

by RHONA CHURCHILL

These letters reveal to the world a secret Rose Macaulay had kept all her life even from her closest friends—the fact that for 20 years she was deeply in love and intimately associated with a married man.

He died during the second world war and there then began for this sensitive woman, born into a High Church background, a long period of remorse and guilt.

Confessor

Her love affair had caused her to lose touch with her Church and with her confessor, Father Johnson of the Cowley Fathers. A chance letter from him, from his priory in Boston, Massachusetts, started up an extraordinary intimate and prolific correspondence which lasted for eight years, up to her death in 1958.

It is clear from the contents of these letters that she took it for granted that the priest would treat them with the same secrecy he applied to conversations in a confessional.

She even wrote asking him to burn them, and promised to burn his letters to her before she died, writing to him : "They're not for other people to see."

She left explicit instructions that any letters not destroyed by her were to be burnt, unread, on her death. This wish was carried out.

What none of Rose Macaulay's friends can begin to understand is why Father Johnson gave his permission to edit and publish them to anyone. He handed them over to Constance Babington Smith, 49-year-old third cousin of Dame Rose, with permission to publish.

The copyright has been vested in her though she was not the residuary legatee, and all royalties will go to her

This is patently a book which should never have been printed. It is in the worst possible taste.

It is claimed that the priest, who died only a few months ago, thought her letters might help others. Yet he was no fool and must have known that it was his replies, not her letters, that might have been helpful, and he knew that she was insisting on these being burnt.

Dame Rebecca West, a close friend of Dame Rose since the first world war, has seen the book and was horrified.

" It made me want to vomit," she told me yesterday. "That this could happen to my dear Rose and against her known wishes fills me with infinite disgust.

" She was a woman of such dignity, fastidiousness, and honesty.

'Burn them'

Another friend, Elizabeth Nicholas, author and journalist, told me : "Publishing these letters is monstrous. I'm certain that Rose thought they would be invested with the absolute security of the confessional.

" It so happens I know exactly what Rose's feelings were about the posthumous publication of letters.

" I was travelling with her on a cruise of the Greek islands. On the last day of the cruise we were sitting alone together in the ship's lounge after lunch.

" I remember the conversation most clearly.

" Dame Rose said : 'Letters should be burnt.'

" I said : ' I've kept all your letters to me.'

" She said : 'Make sure you burn them before you die.'

" Then she said, in her characteristic Rose-like way : 'Letters—real letters—not the notes one writes to the laundry —are intensely personal.

" ' They are written with the understanding they are seen only by the recipient. One says then things one knows the reader will understand, but which would not be the same if read by the public.'"

Elizabeth Nicholas added : "The Rose I knew would writhe at the thought of her letters being published. This dreadful book has exposed to the whole world what was known to very few people and certainly not to me—that for years she was in love with a married man. This she came to regret and repent."

Angered

"I consulted Dame Rose's only surviving close relative, her sister, Jean Macaulay. She agreed with me that the letters should be published.

"I have sent her a copy of the book, and have just had a letter from her saying she is delighted with it."

A spokesman for Collins, who are publishing this book, said yesterday : "We are aware that some of Dame Rose Macaulay's friends are angered by the publication of her letters. But the priest and Dame Rose's sister, her only surviving close relative, have given it their wholehearted support.

"We share Father Johnson's view that publication of these letters may be of great help to many people."

Constance Babington Smith, however, takes the reverse view. "I was not an intimate friend of Dame Rose's," she told me, "for she belonged to an earlier generation. But I knew her. We were third cousins, sharing the same great-great-grandparents. This is why the letters were entrusted to me by Father Johnson.

"He believed that the letters, carefully edited, would be of help to many, and was most enthusiastic that I should tackle the job. He was aware that they were to be published as the letters of Rose Macaulay to him, and not merely the letters of an anonymous woman to a priest. He was perfectly happy with this arrangement.

12. The *Daily Mail* article, 'Did this priest betray this woman?', 12 October 1961.

if it is *of any interest* to anyone else, or whether I'm inventing a weight of significance that it can't carry. Nonetheless, it feels liberating to be doing something that isn't directly life-based – and that no-one else has written about before.

Yesterday Sabina Bowler Reed dropped by on her way back from a court hearing in Weston. She told me there'd been confusion over her invitations to the cruise through the Avon Gorge which she's hosting to celebrate the tenth anniversary of setting up her own law firm. Her secretary, to save time, had addressed the invitations to only one named person of a couple rather than to both; this happened, in almost all cases, to be the woman. A number of them had then rung up in a panic: 'why haven't you invited my beloved husband?' etc. I had simply assumed, incorrectly as it turns out, that it was an old-school feminist women-only event.

9 April

Heard from Mon that she might be able to take time off to come with me to Loughrea in Galway, where Gerald O'Donovan, as Father Jeremiah, was priest many years ago. I hope she can. Research is so much easier with a travelling companion. Meanwhile I spoke on the phone to Father Cathal Geraghty of St Brendan's Cathedral in Loughrea. Apparently in 1996 another priest left, and got married. Father Geraghty: 'I feel quite safe; it obviously only happens once every hundred years.'

The funeral of the Queen Mother has taken place today. People queued up yesterday for five hours and more to 'pay their respects'; much talk of 'thanksgiving' for a full and wonderful life. Those who demurred were trounced as killjoys and being out of touch with the public mood, including one poor newscaster who failed to sport a black tie. The QM left unpaid debts of £7 million; and a fortune in property, works of art etc to members of her family; she kept two cousins locked away in mental hospitals for their whole lives; was a Nazi sympathizer; was so determined to get to the throne that she did everything she could to force Edward's abdication. What did she do for the people? Waved at them from a balcony.

17 April

Can hardly believe how bad my first chapter is – rambling, ill-written, portentous. How did I dare send it to my agent? I've been trying to pull it apart and use some of it for the introduction, and some for the prologue (re Grace's diaries, possibly). On Tuesday I finished teaching an intensive four day 'Writing Our Lives' for the Access Unit. A higher proportion of students than usual were unable to read back their own work; this can be a recipe for disaster, for when a guide reads out the student's work they sometimes lose their invisibility, as it were, and act as if their reading gives them license to interfere in the composition. In my experience, guides who are family members, especially spouses, act particularly heinously in this regard; the blind student feels constrained to write what will please the reading guide. My heart sank when I discovered on Thursday night that two of the guides were family members, one wife and one daughter; but both of them did good work, and in fact the daughter was invaluable, more or less taking dictation, covering page after page of paper while her mother recalled the best days of her life: the blitz of Bristol, and then two years travelling around as an officer in the Wrens. The only man on the course was writing his war memoirs. For neither of these two students had life ever been so intense or sweet.

This morning I woke at 3.20 from a dream in which I had just been handed, along with two or three other objects I can't now remember, a copy of Rose's 1922 novel *Mystery at Geneva*.

Income very low this month – I won't get paid for teaching until the end of next month. Yesterday however I received a cheque from the BBC World Service for £475, for a repeat of my abridgement of Geraldine Brooks's plague novel *Year of Wonders* – a repeat which I hadn't even known about. That cheered me up. And Mon told me she can definitely accompany me to Loughrea. Brilliant! I have booked us tickets to Dublin, and a Hertz car.

22 April

Lunch at the Arnolfini on Friday with Michèle, who had been visiting her mother in Frog Lane. I started talking about my anxieties about the book: about how my interpretations might be wrong, how I've missed things out, how I'm not saying anything new ... and surprised myself by the sudden intense rush of my feelings of despair and inadequacy. I had to struggle to hold back the tears.

On Saturday night I dreamed I was Rose.

❯●

25 April

The introduction, which I had hoped would be concise, snappy, light (but scholarly) etc etc now stands at 7,500 words. I have been moving chunks of it around, forwards, backwards, and just this morning reinstated the opening – the auto-obituary – that had headed the old Chapter One and which I'd moved last week. Difficulties: forcing myself to say why I like Rose and her work and why it's worthwhile reading a new biography of her. In other words, why it's worth my while writing a biography. I have had to drag it out of myself with forceps; then when I read it back it sounds ... lame, limp, banal. Then: making myself deal with other critics' view of her. If I do this here, then I don't need to do it later, so it would be a liberation for me, but even reading anyone, prior to paraphrasing or summing up, fills me with anxiety: that their insights are better than mine, more correct, more insightful ...

❯●

26 April

Late last night I looked for T B (Lord) Macaulay on Google images, to see if I could find a picture that would illustrate Virginia Woolf's 'Lord Macaulay has a look of Rose' – and I did find a cigarette card, dated 1923, of famous men through history, on which he does have a rather Rose-ish look.

❯●

6 May

Dreamed I was in a bookshop in a coastal town and was handed a book by Rose Macaulay that I had never heard of, with a title like *Verucca*. It was no ordinary book, for its pages were stuffed with things to eat, such as olives. I had to wear gloves to turn the pages, but even so my fingers became smeary with olive oil.

Have been reading Denton Welch's *Journals*, which are extraordinarily good. It's just a small patch that he writes about, the village in Kent where he lived, with drinking, bicycling, picnics, passing soldiers and farmhands. Such detail, wonderful detail and a kind of mordant and at times surreal wit that comes from the blackness of his despair at his ruined body. His wildness, his aloneness, his craving for love and the good times he has with Eric Oliver are brilliantly described. I'm reading a copy from the Public Library, and about a third of the way through someone has written in the margin, next to one of the descriptions of a bare-armed and bare-throated farm labourer in a field: 'unhealthy obsession with men'; and about thirty pages later, next to a footnote which says something about Denton Welch 'falling in love' with Eric Oliver, the reader has written: 'ugh, he's queer', and later, next to a sentence about Eric going out to have a 'pee', 'utterly vulgar'. It's bizarre how many pages it took for such a shocked and homophobic reader to realise that Denton Welch was gay. Why do people write their comments? Do they think that other people will find them worth reading? I guess they must do. Or maybe it's just one particular reader, who goes through all the books by gay men in the library and annotates them, starting on about page ten, so that you don't realize they've done it until you've got the book safely home? I seem to remember James Pope-Hennessy's *A Lonely Business* was heavily annotated by a similar – or possibly the very same? – shocked and horrified of Bristol.

These journals are so good because of the way Welch sees and describes the complicated intensity of things, and the way that emotions are never clearcut, but always mixed and contradictory. He remembers being taken out from school when he was eleven: '... we all sat in Ivy Cottage in the pouring rain and listened to the chicken roasting in the oven in the kitchen. The walls of the front room were (and are) panelled in a sort of lincrusta cardboard, and I remember so well the terrible consuming depression and excitement mixed, of the day, the darkness, the good food, the constraint with the elders and the dark threat of returning to school in the evening.' What a brilliant combination and interpenetration of body and soul.

I spoke to Michèle on the phone last night. She thinks the ancestry bits shouldn't be in the introduction, but in another chapter, because the tone of them is so different. It is, I know; but my agent advised me to take them out of Chapter One because they were clogging everything up, so now what? Michèle says: too much detail. She's right. Can the ancestry bits go in later, when Rose starts writing? Going through my notes yesterday I found a message to myself about structure: use the structure of *Told by an Idiot* – Rose's division into Victorian, Fin-de-Siècle, Edwardian – for the pre-First World War chapters. I had completely forgotten.

><•

8 May

Second time round it strikes me as a rather brilliant suggestion.

Chapter Twelve: May 2002

Galway

15 May

My head spins with thoughts of Gerald O'Donovan, and why he left Loughrea, and why he left the church, and why he turned his back on his family background, and why he gave up writing novels, and why, why, why … I don't think I have had to radically re-think anything I knew beforehand, except about poor Mary, Gerald and Beryl's youngest, who died aged twenty-three after swallowing an open safety pin. Muriel had led me to believe she was in some way 'backward', but I discovered she got a place at Cambridge, although she never graduated, which hardly fits with backward. But after talking to John Ryan, and reading all the stuff that he's got, and then talking to Father Geraghty, Gerald's motives seem even more uncertain than they did before, more open to doubt and speculation.

We set off straight for Galway from Dublin airport on Monday morning, driving through heavy rainbursts westwards on the N6. It took me a bit of time to remember and to get used to the Irish roads with the hard shoulder that isn't always a hard shoulder, as it's used sometimes by tractors and sometimes by slow drivers, and sometimes, nerve-wrackingly, has cars parked on it, or women pushing babies in prams. It took only two and a half hours to Loughrea, under a bright blue sky between the storm clouds, with the green land parcelled up by speckled white and grey drystone walls. We booked in at O'Dea's Hotel, which used to be the railway hotel and has the livestock market just behind it. Father Jeremiah O'Donovan's bishop back in the 1890s was called O'Dea. Outside it's painted in red ochre limewash; inside it's cavernous, comfortably tatty, with orange and red and yellow walls. Mrs O'Neill (née O'Dea) the hotelier: 'So, it's Father O'Donovan you're interested in, is it?', her lips set tight and disapproving (or did I imagine that?). 'Well, it's Norman Morgan the printer you'll have to be seeing, he keeps all the data on *that kind of thing*'. What kind of thing? Priests being defrocked? As if it had happened only a few years rather than a whole century ago. First we went to look round St Brendan's Cathedral, where Father O'Donovan was second curate from 1897, when the foundation stone was laid, until 1904, when he left suddenly. Or was it suddenly? I wonder now. Had he been dissatisfied for years?

The presbytery was being whitewashed by eight or ten men in blue overalls up ladders, and there were more workmen inside the church. No lack of money, then. A class of 12- and 13-year-olds was crowded into the front pews in the nave, being coached for their confirmation. The teacher was telling them to stand up straight when their names were called; then they practiced walking in an orderly fashion up to the communion rails. I noticed Mon turning pale – I could tell she was suffering unwelcome convent flashbacks. At least my convent days made up only a small part of my childhood; Mon was convent-educated throughout.

The stained glass: I hadn't realised that only some of the windows were glazed with stained glass in the early 1900s – Sarah Purser's lovely expressive St Brendan the Navigator in the porch, A E Child's three behind the altar – while the rest were installed during the 1920s and 30s, some in the 40s and a rather nice muted St Brigid by Patrick Pye in the 1950s. So: what O'Donovan helped to start went on for half a century. How sad that he never came back to see it. I wonder what Rose thought in 1949 as she looked at the glorious glasswork he had commissioned.

It was time to set off for our appointment with John Ryan in Galway. John wrote his PhD on Gerald, and during the course of his researches became a friend of Mary Anne's aunt Brigid, the O'Donovans' eldest child. More recently John Ryan wrote a monograph: *Gerald O'Donovan: Priest, Novelist and Irish Revivalist*, for the *Journal of the Galway Archaeological and Historical Society*, of which the Rev J O'Donovan had been a founder member. I wanted to take him an offering, but the only shop open in Loughrea was a dusty bakery, which had only one item on display, beneath a dusty glass counter: a dark and possibly dusty porter cake. But better than arriving empty-handed, I thought. We set off westwards, but despite John Ryan's emailed instructions, we were soon hopelessly lost in a dizzying set of turns and roundabouts, and beginning to think the porter cake might turn out a life-saver.

When we finally arrived we found a small, grey-haired, sweet-faced man who, over tea and apple pie and only slightly dusty porter cake, wanted to know why I was writing the book, whether I'd found out anything new, and what was my line on Gerald. I must have said something right because he stood up, said: 'Would you like to see? ....' And proceeded to bring down from his upstairs study ... Beryl's diaries ... Gerald's early love letters to Beryl ... letters from Rose to all three O'Donovan children ... a letter from Marjorie Grant Cook in Canada in 1922 to 'Mr O'Donovan' – hardly the mode of address you'd employ to someone you'd had an affair with, so maybe I'm wrong about *Latchkey Ladies* and the whole Rose/Gerald/Marjorie set-up. John Ryan generously poured these riches into my lap.

Eventually we said we had to go or we'd get nothing to eat for supper. It was late so Mon bravely rang Mrs O'Neill to say we were definitely coming back and would like some supper, please, if that were possible. We arranged to return the following day after we'd seen Father Geraghty. As we left John pressed into my hand a cassette of an RTE programme about Gerald that he'd written and co-produced, and, so that I'd be able to listen to it, his own tape recorder.

In O'Dea's Mon and I dined in solitary splendour on steak, chips, salad and a bottle of St Emilion.

Then I listened to John Ryan's tape. The programme was structured around an interview John conducted with Brigid. I listened to her talking about what an affectionate man her father was, much more affectionate than her mother; she said it was because he came from a large loving family with seven brothers and sisters.

Yet I know that once he'd left Ireland, which was a few years after he left the priesthood, he had nothing more to do with his family. When did the break come? Was it as soon as he gave up being a priest? And did he turn his back on them, or did they chuck him out in shame and anger? A limit to their lovingness, in that case; or their lovingness rejected. And affectionate to his own children? He was disappointed, said Brigid, that his children achieved only third class degrees. That doesn't sound very affectionate to me.

Brigid went on: The children – her and Dermod and poor Mary – weren't allowed to know anything about what their father was doing in case they 'let it out' and the Catholic Church stepped in and wrecked his career, as payback for his leaving the church and writing about it so critically in *Father Ralph*. Gerald was away from home a lot, writing, but they never knew what exactly he was writing or indeed where exactly he was.

How convenient, I thought, for someone conducting an extramarital affair.

I realize I don't very much like Gerald.

Brigid believed that Rose Macaulay and her father were just good friends. She believes it so strongly that I would almost be convinced by her myself were it not for Rose's own testimony to the contrary.

Who – whom, rather – you believe is one of the central questions. My tendency is to believe anyone who isn't obviously lying. As Gerald did to his children and his wife. But it's not always so obvious; nor are the distinctions between knowing and believing, and between believing and wanting to believe, always clear.

Mary Anne was very fond of her aunt Brigid.

First thing next morning Mon and I went to see Norman Morgan. We found him up to his eyes printing a run of programmes for the weekend's music festival in Loughrea, but he was happy to look out what Mrs O' Neill had called 'data on that kind of thing'. All he could find was one photograph of Father O'Donovan in a faded file, which he photocopied for me. O'Donovan holds a priest's hat in one hand, and in the other he holds the hand of a small girl, in ringlets and a white frock, possibly a confirmation girl. He looks much older than thirty-four, which is the last possible time the photo could have been taken. When Father O'Donovan left Loughrea for the last time in 1904, Norman Morgan told us, there'd been a huge farewell party at the station to see him off.

Then we went on to our appointment with Father Geraghty in the priests' house. We waited in the parlour: stiff-backed chairs ranged round the pale green-painted walls; magazines stacked on a low table, all of them, it seemed, with a photo of Padre Pio on their covers; our Lady of Fatima on the dresser. Mon's pallor matched the sickly shade of the walls. Enter Father Geraghty: in his late thirties, plump, and briskly determined to set the record straight, just in case we had been misinformed, on Father Jeremiah O'Donovan and his leaving the parish of Loughrea: O'Donovan preferred 'networking' with the local gentry and intelligentsia to performing his duties as a parish priest; he was bitter about the Catholic church, as can be seen from his novel *Father Ralph*; the people of Loughrea, *especially the nuns*, had been deeply hurt by the way they were portrayed in that book ...

In the Cathedral Museum Mon and I admired the embroidered banners commissioned by Father O'Donovan from Lolly and Lily Yeats, with their mountains and seas glowing blue and green and purple, and the shining golden brown of St Brendan's beard. With a wave of his arm Father Geraghty directed our attention to a series of framed photographs ranked on top of a line of glass display cases which contained ancient ecclesiastical vestments. 'Look, here are photographs of all the Cathedral administrators since the 1890s,' he said. 'All, that is, except Jeremiah O'Donovan.'

Perhaps he sensed our disappointment, for as we took our leave he asked casually:

'And you've seen the photo of Father Jeremiah in the Temperance Hall?'

'No,' I said. 'What photo?'

Back at John Ryan's house in Galway I looked through Beryl's appointment diaries. 'Rose Macaulay to supper,' goes one late 1920s entry, 'Pleasant evening.' And in 1929, Gerald in a letter to Beryl: 'attended a party with Miss Macaulay last night'. At what point did Beryl know about Rose and Gerald? Their children may have believed that Gerald's whereabouts needed to be kept secret from the machinating Catholic hierarchy, but surely Beryl didn't give credence to such a melodramatic tale?

John showed me Beryl's scrapbook. She had pasted into the back cover a cutting of Marghanita Laski's review of *Letters to a Friend*, which starts: 'For 25 years Rose Macaulay had a secret affair with a married man ...'

When I asked John about Gerald's split with his loving (according to Brigid) Irish family, he suggested that Gerald, marrying into the gentry, was perhaps embarrassed by his 'lowly' background.

But if I disapprove of Gerald, for his lying and his secrets, for not loving his children enough and not loving his wife enough, then really

14. The portrait of Father Jeremiah in the Temperance Hall, Loughrea, Galway.

I should disapprove of Rose as well. But I don't. In fact, I admire her. And precisely for those reasons that I disapprove of Gerald. I admire her secrecy. And I admire her passion and her ruthlessness; and her wanting to have it all: the writing, the travelling, the independence, and the consuming love. And, as well, a kind of family life with the O'Donovans: Sunday lunches; doing the crossword with Gerald on Sunday afternoons; and later, being a devoted godmother to the grandchildren. Brigid would only allow the existence of that, last, part of Rose.

The Temperance Hall in Loughrea: cast out from the Cathedral, here is where Father Jeremiah O'Donovan is memorialised, in the old military barracks that he leased from the War Office and opened as a home for the Total Abstinence Society. It was spitting rain by the time Mon and I found it, a substantial three-storey building, with a recent-looking coat of orange paint, set back from the pavement by head-high railings between sturdy stone pillars. A large placard was tied to one section of the railings, advertising an imminent performance in the Hall by the Seamas O'Kelly Players of a play entitled *The Powers That Be*. We followed Father Geraghty's instructions and climbed to the top of the outside stairs, and went in through an unlocked door. The place was deserted. We made our way through a series of empty, bare-boarded, dusty rooms until we found ourselves in the back room that Father Geraghty had described, where an incredibly young-looking Father Jeremiah was hanging unlabelled on the wall, in a baggy jacket with big lapels, looking out over the pages of a book he's holding in both hands.

Did Rose and Marjorie see this photograph, I wonder, when they came on their pilgrimage in 1949? What did they think? What did they say to each other about him? Or was it just Rose, alone, in this deserted building, looking at a young man she had never known, whose very name was different from that of the man with whom she later fell in love? I find it hard to imagine. He remains an enigma to me.

He's remembered all right in Loughrea, but each person's version of him, and of his reasons for leaving, differs. To sum up what I've learned from John Ryan, Father Geraghty, Norman Morgan (and inferred from Mrs O'Neill's basilisk glare): Father O'Donovan was admired by the younger clergy who let it be known that they wanted him as bishop, thus making his position untenable; Father O'Donovan was the only priest the people liked and so his fellow-clergy, jealous of his popularity, drove him out; the people felt neglected because he spent so much time hobnobbing with the gentry and going off on lecture tours. The huge farewell party and the crowds at the railway station? Delighted to see the back of him, they were celebrating his departure; or, the big send-off wasn't just to say goodbye, but to show the remaining priests and the bishop how fond the people were of Father O'Donovan.

An old woman (she must have been extremely old) interviewed by John Ryan for his radio programme remembered Father O'Donovan's good looks and his lively face. 'He was loved and liked in this town and why wouldn't they for what he done in this town?'

Why did he stop writing after *The Holy Tree*? It was his best novel; written, Rose claimed, for her. Perhaps he couldn't sustain writing, and Rose, and his family; perhaps something had to give; or perhaps between the pain expressed in *Father Ralph*, and the passion of *The Holy Tree*, he had written out his soul?

><●

20 May

I had sort of forgotten that this whole pursuit of Rose began with the idea of following in her footsteps to Spain. Which in the end I only did in my imagination in *Thin Woman in a Morris Minor*. Rose herself had the ghost-hunting passions of a biographer. She journeyed in pursuit of ghosts and phantoms, her ears attuned to voices from the past. There is one other place I would like to follow her to: Herrick-country, the Devon of *They Were Defeated*.

><●

25 May

I had been intending to go to my niece's first communion, having decided it would be snooty and unfriendly of me not to go just because I think the sacrament of the body and blood of Jesus Christ is ancient bigotry and mumbo-jumbo. That was before I downloaded from the internet Pius X's 1907 Papal Encyclical against Modernism. I wanted to see what it was that drove Gerald O'Donovan's Father Ralph out of the church and what it meant when people accused O'Donovan of being a 'modernist' (when I first came across this charge against him I thought they meant literary modernism, but of course they didn't). The Encyclical consists of thirty-two pages of diatribe against rational enquiry, against scientific and historical evidence, against the very idea of evidence playing any part in religious belief. It calls down anathema on all who don't believe in God's miracles, anathema on all who raise the tiniest doubts. And then I thought, Father Jeremiah O'Donovan sacrificed his place in a community, his career in a hierarchy, his links with his parents and siblings, in other words his whole life up until then, because he couldn't and wouldn't stomach the Catholic Church's bullying. No, I'm not going to attend a first communion.

Maybe he was snobbish, maybe he didn't love his children enough, or didn't show them he loved them, maybe he deceived his wife and failed in fidelity... but he was a brave man. And an intellectually honest one. And Rose loved him.

Chapter Thirteen:
June–December 2002

Home/London/Home/Dean Prior/London/Home

Thursday June 13

New journal with shiny bright blue cover, bought in the Post Office. I think that 13 June last year was the date of the Arts Council Writers' Award party. And what fun it was, shaking hands with Salman Rushdie, being clapped by a roomful of strangers, congratulated by Judith Murray and Pete Ayrton, and Mum and Dad and Chris being there, and bumping into the other Bristolian award-winner, Matthew Barton. All the poets have doubtless long finished their poetry collections, and the novelists their novels ... and here I am going through Chapter Four, cutting, cutting, rewriting ...

June 14

Email from Diana Hendry, saying she hopes the work-men – putting in a shower and lavatory in the room next to this – aren't playing Radio 2 the whole time. Perish the thought! I made it clear from the start that I was hard at work and absolutely must not be distracted by noise; the only radio that's on is mine, on non-distracting classical Radio 3. Diana's email has now made me feel guilty. But not guilty enough to say they can listen to Radio 2 if they want to. I think Diana's in love with the poet she's met in Edinburgh. I hope so.

Tuesday 18 June

Yesterday I caught the very early morning coach to London for a meeting of the Group of Three, arriving at Queen's Quay at 8.30. We had a fruitful meeting: both Michèle and Jenny are in sight of finishing their novels, and both of them were encouraging about my rewritten

Edwardian chapter. I feel boosted by it, and strong enough now to knuckle down to the Georgian.

><

June 21

I think I am just beginning to make some kind of sense of Rose Macaulay/Rupert Brooke – the fruitfulness for her of being outside his circle, especially in terms of her pre-World War One satires, that is, her sending-up of do-gooding middle-class Fabians in *Views and Vagabonds*, and then of London literary life in *The Making of a Bigot*. Up until now I've been too anxious to disprove that she was in love with him; too worried about what other critics and biographers have said, and feeling I ought to refute their assertions, rather than thinking about how she used Brooke and his circle in her fiction.

The night before last I dreamt someone had suggested a completely brilliant development for the second half of my (still unfinished) play about Dorothy L Sayers, and I think it involved a murder, or at least a corpse. But I didn't write it down when I awoke.

><

Sunday 23 June

Philippa Pearce, with whom I haven't been in touch since last year, rang the other night to alert me to a booklet just published about Barrington, which includes some Conybeare material. Philippa told me that much to her amazement she has started writing again – and has finished the third chapter of a new novel. She thought her fiction-writing days were over, but then suddenly she had this idea, about 'a little gentleman in black velvet' who had lived through three hundred years of English history. I told her how I often think of her and what she said when I first met her, about how one's creative energy flows into one's children. And I remember Janice Galloway, in reply to a question about whether she wrote every day (it must have been at the Hebden Bridge Arvon, where Janice was guest reader), saying, if it's a choice between working on my novel and playing with my wee boy in the garden, of course I play with my wee boy.

><

26 June

It's just as well I decided to put this week aside for preparing for the summer school, as I have had to spend hour after hour on domestic stuff and it would have driven me mad if I were trying to write. It's difficult enough to get through the teaching material. I've managed to read Ricks on Tennyson: clever and readable and very interesting on the poetry: a fine biography; and now in a bit of a panic I've started on Margaret Forster. I'm not enjoying *Hidden Lives* as much as I did the first time round – there's too much Margaret Forster, especially in the second half, and I'm disenchanted with her prose. I must next read *Shadow Baby* and prepare some discussion points, but meanwhile it's Betjeman this morning, who is exasperating but endearing. He's disarmingly frank about his social snobbery and his lusts for the daughters of the aristocracy.

Rose Macaulay doesn't appear in Betjeman's *Letters*, although he writes regularly to and of various of her 1950s friends: Patrick Kinross, Alan Pryce-Jones, William Plomer, and Gerard Irvine. Anyway if he had corresponded with her his letters would have been destroyed after her death in the burning of the papers in her flat. I have just remembered – didn't he too enjoy the high church aesthetics of Grosvenor Chapel? That was where he and she became friends, I think.

Tennyson – Poet Laureate for forty-two years – had another ten years of his long laureateship to run when Rose was born. She grew up knowing him by heart. Her father George had been coached in how to declaim his verse by the great man himself; Tennyson's two sons, Hallam and Lionel, attended George and Grace's wedding in 1878.

Of the three writers I'm teaching this week Margaret Forster is the one with least connection to Rose. I had thought she would be the easiest one for me to prepare, being female and feminist, not to mention contemporary, but it turns out, as she offers no excuse for musing on Rose, she's the one I am most resentful about having to spend the time on.

7 July

Blue and red and yellow striped kites – modern kites that look like quilted mattresses and have no tails – swoop and circle overhead and lead their players in intricate dances over the short grass of Durdham Down. I have just finished, save for the evening session, a whole day's teaching, and have escaped for an hour from the hall of residence.

I didn't quite complete the Georgian chapter this week; I'm still trying to make sense of one of Rose's *Westminster Gazette* poems, and I must incorporate her own comments on the Georgian poets from her Hogarth booklet *Catchwords and Claptrap*, on how they overused words like shimmering, glimmering and honey-coloured moon, and, and ... I know I need to urgently deal with something else but it's been driven out of my head by Margaret Forster. And now jolly John Betjeman is waiting in the wings, ready to bounce into my head and displace even more of my thoughts.

Last night I dreamed Michèle had won two big literary prizes. Here's hoping.

><

10 July

One of my students – partially-sighted rather than blind – left the room yesterday while we were reading and discussing selected extracts from *In Memoriam* ('Ring out, wild bells, to the wild sky ...' George Macaulay would declaim every New Year's Eve to Rose and her brothers and sisters when they were little); I thought she was just going to the loo or needed some fresh air, and discovered only later, at the end of the session, that she had collapsed with a stroke in the corridor and been taken to hospital. Selfishly, my first emotion was relief: that it had happened outside the classroom. Later on we heard she was OK. Her husband was on a walking trip along Offa's Dyke. It took at least three phone calls to get him to abandon it and come to her bedside, and it was with very bad grace that he eventually agreed.

Tennyson yesterday, Betjeman the day before, Clevedon trip today including a visit to the memorial to Arthur Hallam in St Andrew's church. From the grassy graveyard you could hear the rustle of the waves in the Bristol Channel. I recited 'Break, break, break,/On thy cold gray stones, O Sea' but then couldn't remember how it went on (oh for the touch of a vanished hand – I think Rose makes a joke about that somewhere). We agreed that it was hardly likely Lord T was describing the muddy waters of the Bristol Channel, even if his beloved Arthur Hallam was buried here.

Philip Lyons came to give a poetry reading last night, with some excellent new poems, including 'Spike Island', which I commissioned from him for a pint of beer. In the few moments I have off I'm reading Terry Pratchett's *Thief of Time*; not having read Pratchett for a few years now I had forgotten how much I enjoy him. In this one he is very funny on how you become the person you pretend to be: form defining function.

14 July

The course finished late on Thursday night with a quiz organised by specialist staff Pete, who is utterly good-natured but oh so rambling. I would have conducted the quiz in 20 minutes, but with Pete it took an hour and a half. (And possibly for that very reason I have never been invited to act as quizmaster/mistress.) In the final plenary one of the students complained that 'the sessions became dominated by some students'. It was her more than any other student who had tried to dominate every session.

I have been anxious to get back to Rose, and to the rewrite of the *Non-Combatants* chapter, but Friday involved a great deal of driving around, visiting the Access Unit to get the forms signed to ensure I'm paid this month, and shopping because the cupboard was bare. But at last I managed to spend an hour writing up notes on Vera Brittain and felt better as a result.

An email arrived from Judith Murray, passing on an email from Virago: when will the book be delivered? Oh my god I'm only half-way through this draft. Every re-write spawns a further re-write.

17 July

At last I've got hold of Alice Bensen's book on Rose Macaulay, published 1969 in Twayne's English Authors Series. She gives good, careful readings – and I'm rather sorry not to have read it earlier as it offers an alternative to Jane Emery's sometimes overly psychological approach. Perhaps the best way to write a biography is either to not read earlier interpretations at all, or to read all of them right at the very beginning.

Off to London to this year's Arts Council Writers' Awards party – I don't think I've been to a literary party since the one (my one!) last year. I don't know how I would have managed without the £7,000. Well, I wouldn't have. It has made all the difference in the world.

20 July

Excellent party. Jackie Kay was handing out the prizes this year and was incredibly warm and welcoming, as is her nature. Those of my crew from last year who were present didn't seem to have spent the intervening twelve months slaving over a hot manuscript. Pascale Petite: Oh yes, my poetry collection came out last October – I'd more or less finished it when I got the money. She also told me she was fed up with going to so many literary parties. Gerda Meyer (smiley, small, and hard of hearing): I'm only writing my autobiography because then I might be able to sell the 8000 word memoir that I want to sell but no-one will buy. I didn't really want to do anything longer. Oh no, I haven't spent the money – I didn't really need it.

At which point I decided not to approach any of my other co-winners.

When I got home there was an email from Paul S telling me I'll get only half the teaching money this month because someone (someone?) failed to sign the second form that authorises payment. The usual humiliating grovelling at the bank ensued, then I fell into a slough of despond. Must just grit the teeth (but not too forcefully, as the dentist suggests that that's why I've been getting toothache), finish the book, and then try hard to get more regular work.

23 July

My old Chapter Seven has become a new – and I hope improved – Chapter Five. Why didn't I write the book in a straightforward chronological way in the first place? Perhaps I was trying too hard to emulate Hermione Lee's rather brilliant thematic approach to Virginia Woolf – but it hasn't worked for me. Re-reading Five (Seven) today, I keep on finding 'Rose *had* done this, *had* felt that ...'. The horrible distancing pluperfect, and a complete muddle as to the order of some pretty straightforward events: the outbreak of war, the death of Rupert Brooke, Rose taking on hateful VAD work, the death of her father.

The VAD work: it must have been at Mount Blow, early in 1915, that she heard stories of what it was like in the trenches – surely it was too early for it to be common knowledge to the general public? The descriptions of trench warfare in *Non-Combatants and Others*, which she began writing while she was VADing, sound utterly authentic. And Alix's sick horror at it all was very likely an expression of Rose's own sick horror. Did she have some kind of breakdown? Exacerbated by the death of her adored father? It does seem extraordinary that she was incapable – physically, mentally? – of attending his funeral. This has become a series of breakdowns: 1903, 1909, 1915, 1919. What form did they take? Did she retire to her bed? Fall silent? Weep uncontrollably?

30 July

Paul Fussell's book on the Great War and memory is just fantastic. I want to read it slowly to savour all the fascinating points, all the ironies he teases out in the writings that he quotes. But there's nothing – needless to say – on Rose; for lots of these male writers it's as if she never existed.

I had thought that I had finished and put to bed Rupert Brooke in the last chapter, and in this one only had to say RB d April 1915 – but, oh no, here are Rose and Rupert together again on the same page in *Poems of Today*, here they are both of them writing about death and flowers and suns and drifting dust. Fussell writes interestingly about Brooke's dawns and sunsets.

2 August

Did the First World War male poets tend to make all their women mothers? While women, writing of the war, peopled their poems with sisters?

10 August

The 1920s chapter was considerably thinner and scrappier than I remembered, and was built on what I now recognise as my usual weird pattern of hopping around here and there and too much repetition. In the early 1920s Rose writes two realistic descriptions of morning sickness and pregnancy, in *Potterism* and in *Crewe Train*. Of course she might easily have got details from someone else (Marjorie Grant Cook, for example?!).

I'm struggling to thicken it all up and give it a more coherent structure. Last week was rather disjointed – I had to do loads of driving, and then was disturbed by sinister movements from next door involving the delivery of truckfuls of gravel and stone. The sight of Mr NextDoor's angry face peering at me from behind the wheel as he rockets down the drive – I know now the true meaning of the phrase 'his face was twisted in hate' – makes me feel sick in the stomach.

14 August

I have just re-read *Crewe Train* and I think my original interpretation is not quite right. Denham's stubborn anti-intellectualism makes her more of a comic rather than a tragic figure.

Dreamt last night that I was catching a train with Mum from King's Cross, which had CREWE written on it on the inside of the door. Although it was the Crewe train, it was going instead to Crewkerne. Mum got on and I had to gather up all our bits from the platform: her hat-box, my open bag, and various pairs of shoes. As soon as I picked up one pair, I'd notice another one: my pale purple high-heels, the red Italians, my leather sandals, and then I noticed my wedding shoes. I bundled them into my arms and tried to shove them onto the Crewe train behind Mum.

25 August

Lennie Goodings sent jacket proofs: the two pictures of Rose as a young woman, front and back, tinted up in pinks and greens. I think it looks lovely – with Rose-coloured lettering for her name and curlicues on the 'o' and 'u'. It looks feminine, and I like it, not least because I see it as illustrating the hidden femininity I write about.

Now the jacket's nearly ready I had better hurry up and finish writing the book.

I dreamt last night C had picked up and read two of my chapters in typescript, and said he thought they were very good.

28 August

I took the manuscript round to Sara Davies last night, as she's going up to London to see Lennie on Radio 4 business, and kindly offered to deliver it for me by hand. And I sent half of a second copy to Judith Murray – the last four chapters are printing now. I cannot believe how long it has taken to do this rewrite – I've been working almost non-stop since the beginning of the summer, starting at 8.15 or 8.30 each morning, and going on until eleven at night. Stopping of course for shopping, cooking, ferrying. But it's far from finished, for as I end each chapter with a long list of queries to myself, things to put in, bits to take out, I have the nightmarish thought that I could go on writing and rewriting it for ever. And I've just realised that I haven't yet read all the way through non-stop, but only one chapter at a time. I should read all the way through before I go back to the introduction. Writing the damn thing leaves no time for reading it.

Note to self: Next time embrace the structure offered by the chronology of a person's life right from the beginning. 'Next time' – what an exhausting prospect!

6 September

I suddenly felt an urgent need to deal with the introduction – partly because Lennie rang and innocently asked for it, and I thought well, of course, the introduction is needed as that is what it is, an introduction to what comes. And I was cheered up by Lennie who said she could tell just by glancing at the manuscript how good it was. Oh clever, clever Lennie! I don't think that back in the days of The Women's Press I was half as good and encouraging an editor as she is. So I thought, well, I'll just have a look at the introduction, which I did on Friday, and with the help of Michèle's and Diana's comments from three months ago, I ruthlessly cut all the boring historical bits where I rant on about Victorianism and empire and the rise of the middle-class; I cut the auto-obituary (which I'll put in later, in the 1930s chapter, where it belongs) which I had mentioned to Lennie as a locus of anxiety, and which she said (oh clever Lennie) she thought might not be right in the introduction, and then, at last, I wrote down, as Diana had suggested: Emilie Rose Macaulay was born on ... in ..., and it was all over and done with in a paragraph, what I had been anguishing over for months. Saturday and Sunday I spent scrubbing, dusting, wiping, cleaning the room for Eva, who arrives from Germany next week to spend the autumn term with us and go to school with HB. Then on Monday I finished the notes to the introduction, and sent it off on Tuesday.

I have arranged a trip to Dean Prior next Thursday, to visit Pat Baker, who lives in Keeper's Cottage, home to Dr Conybeare and his talented daughter Julian in *They Were Defeated*, I think possibly my favourite of all Rose's novels. Tessa has promised to come with me.

I know I ought to ring Veronica Babington Smith, Constance's niece and inheritor of the rights in her and Rose's estates, and arrange to go and see her in Oxford. I'm worried she might be difficult, and as a result keep on putting off picking up the phone.

><>

9 September

Reading Samuel Hynes on the 1930s, interesting and well-written of course, but so far the only woman mentioned is Naomi Mitchison.

Bizarre how intelligent men like Hynes and Fussell can be so blind to women.

The pleasures of reading for pleasure: I don't do enough of it at the moment. I read Reginald Hill's *Dialogues of the Dead* about three weeks ago, and this weekend thought I would treat myself to the sequel, *Death's Jest Book*. He is reliably entertaining, never dull. And Daniel Handler's *The Basic Eight*, a teen scream with a wildly unreliable narrator and a marvellous absinthe-poisoning sequence. Handler is aka Lemony Snicket.

><

14 September

To Dean Prior on Thursday with Tessa. We stopped first at Keeper's Cottage in Deancombe, which is the very house that Rose gave to atheistical Dr Conybeare and his daughter Julian the poet in *They Were Defeated*, and now belongs to 89-year-old Pat Baker, founder member of the Herrick Society. She gave us coffee and biscuits and then the three of us drove over to the other side of the Devon Expressway – the dual-carriageway A38 – which runs slap along the middle of the valley and splits the village in two, cutting off Dean Prior church – Herrick's church – and the squire's house Dean Court from the houses and cottages of the village. Apparently two parishioners were run over a couple of Christmases ago as they turned out into the road from the church. Squire Yarde lives in Dean Court in *They Were Defeated*; they drag the poor old suspected witch Mother Prowse there after they've found her hiding in Dr Conybeare's cottage. We stopped and met the current lady of the manor who talked about the difficulties of maintaining such an old house, and how the Jacobean screen in the dining hall was impossible to clean.

In the church I pictured the opening scene of the novel: a Harvest service with Herrick chiding his parishioners from the pulpit while below him, hidden from his sight, but keeping the congregation agog with merry expectation, a piglet munches its way through a heap of melons and pumpkins and apples.

When we came back to Keeper's Cottage I went down to the bottom of the lane and walked back up reading the passage in the novel where

Julian comes over the high fields from the church with Meg and Giles Yarde, crosses the brook – which I'd already seen bubbling along at the bottom of Pat's garden – and walks up to the grey stone cottage. It fits exactly. Then on up the lane to the moor, from where you can see Dean Wood crawling up the valley, and where Rose must have stood seventy-one years ago, looking at the landscape she would so lovingly describe. She had just turned fifty.

Pat's going to look up the church visitors' book for me – it's locked away and now she's resigned from the PCC she no longer has a key – to see if Rose signed it in 1931. As I'm sure she would have.

Just as we approached the turn-off from the M5 on the way home, Tessa and I heard an odd noise on the road surface. I didn't want to stop on the hard shoulder, but luckily basic instinct overrode desire, and I'd already started to pull over when the tyre burst. Any faster and I don't think I would have had any control at all over the steering. We stopped and got out. Smoke spiralled up from the shredded remains of the tyre. My legs were shaking and I couldn't speak. But Tessa was a tower of strength – with mobile, AA card, and calm.

✦

25 September

Pat Baker sent me a copy of the page where Rose signed her name in the Dean Prior church visitors' book. R Macaulay, no date; the visitor above dated 6 October 1931. It was here when I got back from London last night, after two days of unbelievably stressful driving. Four and a quarter hours to get to the newspaper library at Colindale, and four and a quarter hours back yesterday. Every time you think you can get up some speed, it lasts about two minutes and then you're in another jam. At least parking was easy at the library as you can use the big mental hospital car park over the road, where they charge only £1 for three hours. As for the people in the newspaper library, well, they looked as if they might have come from over the road too – I know public libraries remain one of the few havens for the homeless, and I seemed to be the only reader not wearing a food-stained T-shirt, and the only one not determined to avoid eye contact (although being singular in this regard meant of course that I didn't make eye contact with anyone). A big black man was reading bound volumes of knitting magazines, chuckling quietly as he turned the pages; a fat white man on the microfilm machine behind me seemed to be researching stories about paedophiles and perverts in the popular press. The fiddling you have to do with the machines: half the time they won't take up the film that you've carefully fed in according to instructions, and you have to go and get a man from the desk, who comes with a pair of scissors and snips off the frayed end of the tape. So it all takes an age, but I did find the *Daily Chronicle* article from 1912 with the photo of Rose looking, as she herself said 'remarkably like me' – she's clear-eyed, regular-featured, unfussy, very different from the photos of other women, who all look so Edwardian with their hats and frills and wavy hair and soupy expressions. Rose looks astonishingly modern by contrast. I didn't get round to *Time and Tide* because I had to go off and do *Saturday Review* stuff (a crash underneath the Marylebone Flyover was creating further chaos, so that was nerve-wracking as I was so anxious not to be late); I shall have to return.

28 September

Two more days in London. This time I went by train. From leaving home to Colindale it took four and a half hours – but at least I was able to read Claire Tomalin's biography of Pepys on the train. She's such a good biographer – present in the book, but not obtrusively so. Only the first three years of *Time and Tide* are on microfilm, thank God. I hate reading on microfilm. Because the first one I read, 1921, lacked an index, I had to stop, fast forward, stop, fast forward, stop, and after about half an hour I began to feel incredibly sick. And just like carsickness, it doesn't go away, even when you stop reading. This was worse than carsickness, because you're stuck in a dark claustrophobic cell, and there's always a bit of the page that's out of focus anyway, and it's very difficult to write notes because the light – a horrid neon-type light – falls over your shoulder so you have to write in the shadow of your own hand. It was a relief to get to the bound volumes.

3 October

Some time ago I requested through interlibrary loan a copy of Hugh Walpole's story collection *All Souls' Night*, to check it out for its dedication to Rose Macaulay and Sylvia Lynd. Since then I've been in correspondence with the Walpole Librarian at the King's School in Canterbury – there are a couple of postcards from Rose in the collection – who sent me the details of the Walpole Bequest, and confirmed the dedication. Yesterday, in Chichester, going through C's aunt Sheila's books to clear the house, and dividing them into volumes we definitely don't want (Generals' memoirs, books of etiquette, sayings of Popes) and others we might want (concordances and encyclopedias), I came across a small cache of Georgian and 1920s publications – which I guess came from Sheila's father who was editor of the *Pall Mall Gazette* – and in it was a copy of *All Souls' Night*. The only Walpole there! Dedicated to 'Two Wise Women: Rose Macaulay and Sylvia Lynd'. While driving home across the dark and misty Mendips, the punning nature of the dedication suddenly struck me. Robert Lynd signed his weekly *New Statesman* articles 'YY': 2 Ys: too wise. Could Walpole be making a joke about that? '2 Ys' women'?

It made me reflect on how odd it was that Rose, so English, so cool and reticent, should have been attracted to not just one but to *two* passionately nationalist Irishmen: one an ex-priest, the other the son of a protestant minister.

><>

6 October

Mary Beard, in the *London Review of Books*, on the reception in 1952 of Gwen Raverat's *Period Piece*, shamelessly manipulates (I guess manipulation is always shameless) her readers' judgements. Most reviewers, she writes, 'gushed with sentimental enthusiasm ... Rose Macaulay, for example, oozed – anonymously – in the *Times Literary Supplement* 'an altogether delightful book ..." 'Anonymously' implies something dishonest. But all *Times Literary Supplement* reviews were anonymous then, as Mary Beard must know perfectly well. And why 'gushed' and 'oozed'? Why not 'enthused', or simply 'wrote' or 'said'? She goes on to say that someone else 'chimed in', thus creating an impression of some kind of cosy pro-Raverat conspiracy. But her interpretation isn't borne out by the evidence, which shows nothing more than that Rose Macaulay and a number of other reviewers very much liked the book.

What would be interesting is *why* they very much liked it. Gwen Raverat, like Rose, grew up in the last years of Victoria's reign, and, like Rose, was allowed extraordinary physical freedoms: Gwen cycling home at night on her own aged eleven, Rose scrambling barelegged up Italian hillsides. From *Period Piece*: 'I wanted so much to be a boy that I did not dare to think about it at all, for it made me feel quite desperate to know that it was impossible to be one. But I always dreamt I was a boy. If the truth must be told, still now, in my dreams at night, I am generally a young man!' (Raverat 1952, 129). It makes me think of Rose's ambition to become a naval captain, and of all the boyish young women who saunter through her novels.

Mary Beard's is an easy rhetorical trick. I could do it myself: "Most reviewers gushed with sentimental enthusiasm,' sneered (or sniped, or grumbled) Mary Beard in the *London Review of Books*'. Her critical judgment would thus be undermined by the imputation of bad temper. I was surprised: the question of intellectual honesty was at the heart of her brilliant – I thought – book on Jane Harrison.

><•

14 October

The phone rang on Friday evening and it was Polly Gaster, saying her cousin Nancy wanted to get in touch with me but had lost my email address and phone number, and so had contacted Polly in Maputo, and Polly, over in London for Jack Gaster's 95th birthday party (200 guests at Hampstead Town Hall, all organised by Jack, and a speech given by him), had rung around various people to get my number. And why did Nancy want to get hold of me? She was going through some stuff last week at the request of a professor from York who was pursuing a Lynd connection with T S Eliot, and she found ... a small paper bag containing about 70 letters from Rose to Sylvia. I rang Nancy at once, and have arranged to go round on Wednesday morning. She said the letters look like general chit-chat. I said, 'Fine'.

Woke up this morning feeling very sick. Still no money from the BBC, despite having finished the abridgement of Paul Richardson's *Indulgence* two weeks ago. Perhaps I feel sick with rage at the BBC – or perhaps I feel sick because of drinking too much wine yesterday.

><

18 October

Nancy very kindly provided me with bread and cheese and fruit for lunch, and tea and coffee at regular intervals ...

I think that Rose really really liked Sylvia Lynd. The letters move on swiftly from formality ('Dear Mrs Lynd') in the early 1920s – literary arrangements, invitations to her and Mr Lynd to a Thursday evening at 44 Princes Gardens as Mr O'Donovan would like to meet them – to 'dearest Sylvia' and 'my dearest Sylvia' and warm expressions of affection, along with concern for Sylvia's chronic ill health. Much mild literary gossip: the ghastliness of Clemence Dane (Rose hates her 'fluting womanly tones'); the paranoia of Naomi Royde-Smith (poor Naomi – she and Rose had been good friends in earlier years), who thinks Rose has bribed reviewers to not review Naomi's novels; Hugh Walpole's worries about what books he should or shouldn't admire.

Rose sent Sylvia a series of postcards from the American trip in 1929 where she extols the joys of driving down the Pacific Highway. I think perhaps I was completely wrong about Rose learning to drive as a young woman in Wales – that the 'driving veil' made for her by her elder sister Margaret in 1906 was for driving a carriage, not a car. Well, I put the youthful Rose driving a car in Wales into *Thin Woman in a Morris Minor*, which has now been broadcast twice so too late to change it. How easy it is to make mistakes! Now that I think about it I realize that the references in Margaret's Wales diary are all to her and Rose walking and bicycling. Maybe the family had a horse and carriage. I'd just never thought about it very much.

When Luxborough House was bombed Sylvia invited Rose to go and stay with the Lynds in Keats Grove, and when Rose declined the invitation Sylvia sent her a present of four pairs of stockings.

Rose wrote to Sylvia the day after Gerald O'Donovan's funeral in 1942, saying how she had had the best of Gerald, that their love hadn't been worn away or spoiled by domestic life. She wrote about how he and Beryl had long ago stopped loving each other, and how he had not wanted Beryl in his room as he lay dying. Is this true? Rose doesn't mention the presence at Gerald's bedside of Marjorie Grant Cook, although the O'Donovan family story relates that Marjorie was specifically invited as an old family friend to nurse Gerald in his last days. Now I come to think of it, that seems a bit unlikely, too. I mean Marjorie Grant Cook hadn't done any nursing since 1918 for heaven's sake! She was a novelist and a literary critic!

Rose writes to Sylvia about how she 'would like to have had one or two children of his' but it would have been too 'complicated'. 'Twenty four years of companionship, unspoilt. Perhaps it was mean – eating the butter and jam and leaving the dry bread to others. I don't know. But one can't help feeling glad we had it, and have it.' These ambivalent feelings about adulterous love – the selfishness and the joy – she'll give to Laurie fourteen years later in *The Towers of Trebizond*. Then Rose gives a long description of how that night (ie the night before she's writing the letter) J C Squire (about whom she and Sylvia had often made unkind jokes) had come round to her flat the worse the wear for drink, had left a taxi ticking outside, and had wept at the news of the death of Rose's cousin and his old friend Donald Macaulay – who had died a year ago, but Squire hadn't realised – and Rose saying to Sylvia it should have been her who was weeping. Naturally J C Squire knew nothing about Gerald. Just as Lees-Milne knew nothing when on the first anniversary of Gerald's death, when he and Rose were guests at a dinner party given by Una Pope-Hennessy, he coldly wrote of her in his diary as being 'dry and twitchy'. Keeping your grief a secret must be more difficult – and more damaging – than keeping your love a secret. The burden of Rose's secret grief stopped her writing novels.

><>

9 November

I feel as if I'm crawling from day to day with a huge heavy sack on my back.

><>

13 November

I sent the two final chapters, and the epilogue – the story of the furore around Constance's publishing of Rose's letters to Father Hamilton Johnson ('that rat-faced priest' according to Elizabeth Bowen, quoted in Wilson 1992, 147), off to Lennie yesterday. I haven't yet done the notes for the last chapter. Nor for the introduction, which I ought to do soon, before I forget what I've taken out of it and put elsewhere, and won't be able to find without re-reading the whole manuscript, which would take me another three days at least. But I must now do the Radio 4 abridgement of Tracy Chevalier's *Girl with a Pearl Earring* which I should have started on Monday. I came to download it this morning from its attachment – but the attachment appeared to have vanished – aargh! I should have checked it as soon as it arrived ten days ago but I just didn't want to have anything else in my head except Rose.

18 November

Someone from Virago rang on Thursday afternoon saying they needed the notes for chapter ten and the epilogue in order to send them to the copy-editor. So I had to put aside *Girl with a Pearl* and do the notes – which I finished at 1 am, sent off first thing Friday morning, then went back to the abridgement. Felt utterly weary by Friday night.

21 November

While working on a final draft of *Girl with a Pearl* in the light of the changes (good changes) Sara Davies had suggested at our meeting on Monday, I managed to do some little bits and pieces on Rose, such as writing a formal letter to the literary agency that controls her estate with a request for permission to quote for a nominal fee. Which brought to mind that when I was re-writing my 1950s chapter I dug out my copy of Rose's will that I'd got last year from the Public Records Office, and when I looked at it again it struck me that Rose appears to have left all her copyrights to the 'Public Trustee', and to her sister Jean only the royalties in her published work. Which is rather different – I think, but I'm not completely sure – from leaving all copyrights to Jean, and Jean leaving them to Constance Babington Smith, and then them being passed to Constance's niece. What exactly does 'Public Trustee' mean? Does it mean, I wonder, that the control of Rose's estate never, legally, rested with Constance? If Constance never had legal control, by what right is Box 12 in the ERM archive in the Wren Library closed until 2012? Oh my goodness.

28 November

Months ago, daydreaming about what it would be like to actually finish the book, I imagined brushing its hair and cleaning its shoes and sending it off like a child on her first day at primary school, and while you might feel an agony of separation you would soon move on to the next phase of your life, and the book/child would become sturdily independent. Well, it's not like that at all. Today the typescript was returned by the copy-editor with eight pages, in tiny eight-point, of comments and queries. I obviously hadn't brushed its hair sufficiently thoroughly, and its shoes are still scuffed. Meanwhile I'm seeking permission to quote and to use photos, and wishing I had done this as I went along, before I mislaid half the names and addresses of the copyright owners.

15 December

I think finishing a book is more like getting a divorce than like sending a child out into the world; and least of all like giving birth. Endless niggling details have to be discussed backwards and forwards, letters of supplication written to Random House, saying no I can't afford such and such an amount for quoting just three lines of Virginia Woolf, and letters of protestation to the Wren at what they want to charge for reproducing some of the Macaulay family photos. Where are the feelings of pride, or relief? I'm filled with anxiety and frustration, tied by a hundred tiny ties to the book I want to cast off.

22 December

Last night, just before I fell asleep, I read the exchange in Anthony Powell's *Temporary Kings* between Ada Leintwardine and Nick Jenkins over control of the rights in and the royalties accruing from the St John Clarke estate. Ada – whose own success as a novelist took off with *Bedsores* and *The Bitch Pack Meets on Wednesday* – suggests that it was 'for the sake of tidiness' that the publishers Quiggin & Craggs acquired the rights in St John Clarke's books, being already the beneficiaries of his royalties through the Warminster Trust. St John Clarke had left the royalties, but not the rights, to Warminster. I'm now feeling confused about the right of Constance Babington Smith to control the rights in Rose's writings. I'm beginning to think that maybe Jean and Constance never did have control of Rose's literary estate, although they both definitely thought they did. But, after all, they passionately believed that Rose's letters to father Hamilton Johnson would be read as an uplifting story of forgiveness and reconciliation with the church. And they could hardly have been more wrong about that.

Later I dreamed about Constance – a young and beautiful Constance in pearls as she appears on the jacket flap of her biography, and sporting a hat that I knew in the dream was the bomber hat she'd made herself, although it looked like the Russian-spy-style beret that Rose was wearing in the photo the *Daily Mail* printed alongside their screaming headline 'Did this priest betray this woman?' when Constance's edition of Rose's letters to Hamilton Johnson first appeared. Constance was watching me as I planted scarlet geraniums in a raised brick bed outside a block of flats – Duchess of Bedford House in Kensington – where I used to go and stay with Aunt Dolly when I was little. But I realize now: I wasn't me. I was Rose.

Chapter Fourteen: Endings, 2012

Home/Cambridge

Wednesday 6 June

Slim blue notebook with the pale skeleton of a leaf (a birch leaf perhaps?) glued to its stiff matt front cover. It comes from the Paradise Road Company – did Jenny Newman give it to me, or do I think that because of the delicate leaf-skeleton candle-holder she gave me last year? A new notebook for my final biographical encounter with Rose Macaulay.

During the course of revising and rewriting this journal I have thought every so often about pursuing the question of whether Constance Babington Smith ever really had any rights over Rose's correspondence. Early on I made some enquiries of a law firm specialising in artistic copyright, but their answer – as so often with lawyers' answers – wasn't unequivocal. Other work and other books subsequently intervened and, asking myself, does it really matter?, I pursued it no further. And now the fifty-year embargo placed by Constance on the originals of Rose's letters to the Anglican priest Hamilton Johnson is about to be lifted. Next week, on Tuesday, the sealed box will be unsealed! Not that it was actually sealed when I was last in the Wren Library in Trinity College, Cambridge, nearly a decade ago. Meanwhile, control of the Rose Macaulay estate has passed, since the death a couple of years ago of Constance's niece Veronica Babington Smith, to the Society of Authors.

So next Monday evening in Cambridge I'm meeting Martin Ferguson Smith, prior to our both turning up at the Wren at 9 am the following morning, 12 June 2012, fifty years to the day since Constance imposed her embargo. Martin Ferguson Smith is Emeritus Professor of Classics at Durham and editor of Rose's letters to her cousin, his aunt, Jean Smith (published last year as *Dearest Jean*). Jean Smith was one of those who, like so many of Rose's friends and relations (such as Rose's uncle Edward, vicar of Barrington), 'went over', as they used to say, to Rome. On the Thursday we'll be joined by Dr Lara Feigel from King's College,

London, who's got a book coming out on five London writers of the interwar years, of whom Rose Macaulay is one.

Over the last week I've been rereading the two volumes of Rose's letters to Hamilton Johnson. They were published in 1961 and 1962, as *Letters to a Friend* and *Last Letters to a Friend*. In her prefaces Constance Babington Smith tells us that when she received the bundle of correspondence from Hamilton Johnson he had made three deletions. Constance herself has omitted references to living persons where she thinks it might cause embarrassment; omissions that she's marked, along with Hamilton Johnson's deletions, with a three-dot ellipsis. I've been noting them all with blue (Vol 1) and yellow (Vol 2) Post-it slips, which now bristle in alarming profusion out of the top of each book. The most frequent contexts for Constance's ellipses appear to be: Graham Greene; a promiscuous young woman friend of Rose's; Rose's recurring undulant fever; and various books and priests.

In the final letter of the first volume Rose tells Hamilton Johnson: 'I think you'd better get rid of [the letters], of any you have kept, in that incinerator!' Constance, in her preface to the second volume, tells us that on Rose's instructions her sister Jean Macaulay burned all the letters Rose had received, and goes on insouciantly: 'Dame Rose did not, however, leave instructions of any kind banning the publication of letters written by herself.'

><>

7 June

In Michael Holroyd's playful, personal, elegiac book about Eve Fairfax, Violet Trefusis, and the Villa Cimbrone, *A Book of Secrets: Illegitimate Daughters, Absent Fathers*, which I've been reading over the last couple of days, he writes: 'Biographers often struggle to escape the prison of chronology before resigning themselves to opening with a birth.' (He goes on: 'Violet Keppel was born in London on 6 June 1894', Holroyd 2010, 141.) That's what happened with Rose, after I'd been flailing around for months trying to find a starting-point and thus a structure. In my Samora Machel biography I started with his death, which seemed obvious as soon as I'd done it because it suggested a thriller-type structure as a response to the question: who killed him? But it wasn't obvious to me beforehand. How many writers, I wonder, feel that they learn something from each book they write, and how many feel, as I do, that each time they have to start again from scratch?

Reading *Letters* (and *Last Letters*) *to a Friend* and noting the omissions made by Constance and by Hamilton Johnson makes me reflect on the omissions I have made in this biographical journal: I have cut out what I consider to be other people's stories if I have felt unable (through not knowing whoever-it-is well enough, or through not wanting to be in touch with them because I don't like them, or through judging the stories to be potentially hurtful or humiliating) to ask for permission to include them. Which, it strikes me now, stands in stark contrast to the driving purpose of a biography, which is precisely to tell other people's stories, and especially those of people that you don't personally know (because they're dead); and to include everything that adds to the pattern of your narrative, irrespective of what that person might have found hurtful or humiliating.

And, realising that I would rather not have any of my passing ill humour preserved in the aspic of publication, I have cut out a handful of casual cruelties. With regret in some cases, especially when I reflect on how a clear, unloving eye animates a good diarist such as James Lees-Milne. Lees-Milne wasn't afraid to show his heartlessness.

At the end of Rose's fourth letter to Hamilton Johnson, dated 27 November 1950, Constance Babington Smith has written in square brackets: *The next page of this letter was missing when the correspondence was received from Father Johnson.* Will we find the missing page floating in the 'sealed' box? I wonder momentarily, and then think, no. Constance would never have lied. (Had she been dishonest she would surely have inserted three dots to replace Rose's sentence suggesting Hamilton Johnson throw her letters in his incinerator.)

Hamilton Johnson's first editorial intervention (after the missing page of Rose's fourth letter) occurs in the ninth letter in the collection, dated 9 January 1951. Constance's ellipsis indicates Johnson's deletion; it's quite impossible to deduce any clues from the context. By the 28th of the same month Rose is exploring the meaning, or consequences, of her relationship with Gerald O'Donovan. O'Donovan is not named in the two volumes, but Rose refers to him as early as in her second letter to Hamilton Johnson, where she calls him 'the man I loved' in a list of names she prefaces with: 'The people I love most have died.' In her 28 January letter she writes: 'Not all the long years of happiness together, of love and friendship and almost perfect companionship (in spite of its background) was worth while, it cost too much, to us and to other people. I didn't know that before, but I do now. And he had no life after it to be different in, and I have lived the greater part of mine. If only I had refused, and gone on refusing. It's not a question of forgiveness, but of irrevocable damage done. Perhaps I shall mind more and more all my life. Is this what absolution and communion do to one? I see now why belief in God fades away and has to go, while one is leading a life one knows to be wrong. The two can't live together.'

I had forgotten quite how early on in the correspondence occur Rose's confession and – we must assume, as we don't have the other side of the correspondence – Hamilton Johnson's absolution (or as Constance's Roman Catholic critics would have it, the 'confession' and 'absolution'). This one, the letter of 28 January 1951, is the fourteenth out of nearly two hundred (one hundred and ninety-nine, to be precise). If what Rose wrote here was considered by Constance to be fit for publication, what on earth are all the deletions going to consist of? There's surely nothing left to confess (or 'confess')?

Monday 11 June: Pembroke College, Cambridge

A student room on the first floor of Pembroke's light-filled modern building, Foundress Court. The corridor has internal glass walls around an inner courtyard with a small pool and a dark-leafed evergreen in a stone garden. Light pours in, and also through the floor-to-ceiling glass of the kitchens in the crook of each storey's L. The building's Japanese architect won an award, I'm told. I suspect the huge-windowed rooms might get pretty hot in the summer. In a normal summer, that is. The window of the room I've been given (I guess its usual occupant must have finished his or her exams and gone away for a week or two) is shaded by one of the majestic plane trees that guard the avenue leading to the back gate of the College, and through its windswept branches I can see chinks of dull grey sky. The room is spacious enough but the bed looks to me like a mere narrow cot in the corner. The shower and lavatory are down the corridor. I have grown unaccustomed to communal living. And to small beds.

I used to stay with Sheila Stern when I came to work in the Wren, but she died in 2005. The house in Barton Road, designed by her and J P Stern when they came to Cambridge in the early 1950s, with its garden sloping down to the secret lake, was sold soon after her death. I'm going to miss her tales of academic intrigue, and the beneficent dry martinis she would mix for us when I used to stagger in, dizzy from a long day of reading and note-taking.

Sheila's not the only person who is no longer around. I'm also thinking about my dad, who died in 2004, the year after my biography of Rose came out. He was here at Pembroke in 1939 and then again, on his return from the War, in 1945. All the undergraduates were men, of course. How strange it must have been to return to these ancient peaceful courts after five years of war. Many of them didn't return: their names are carved into the cloister walls outside the chapel, past which I earlier dragged my ridiculously heavy suitcase.

Out to dinner with Professor Martin Ferguson Smith this evening, at his invitation, to the Cambridge Chop House on King's Parade. He was dressed in tweed jacket and neatly pressed fawn chinos, and was courteous, old-school. He appeared anxious about how we're going to read the letters, that is, the practicalities of doing so; we'll have to follow the Wren protocol of separately receiving each set of letters from the librarian in charge and then handing them back before the other person can have them. I told him I'd be happy to take the second bundle while he read the first. Look, Martin, I wanted to say, it doesn't matter who gets to read them first. I don't care!

➤●

Tuesday 12 June: 9 am

On the trolley beside the scholars' desk, beyond marble Lord Byron on his plinth, sat the sealed box. Already unsealed. The lid showed the scars of a few generations of brown tape, framing a note in red biro, stuck on with some strips of newish-looking tape: CLOSED FOR 30 YEARS: UNTIL 1 JUNE 2012. Inaccurate on both counts. Were I driven by competition I could have stolen a march on the Professor and turned up twelve days ago.

The duty librarian (I remember him from ten years ago) took out the first two paper folders of letters and after some jockeying of 'after you' and 'no, after you', I insisted on the final 'after you' and Martin took the first bundle while I took the second. At a glance, I felt huge relief to see that most of the letters were typewritten, many of them on airmail forms; the only handwritten script squashed into the spaces above and around the greeting. The letter containing the first of Hamilton Johnson's deletions, Rose's ninth letter, was in Martin's bundle; we pulled our chairs close to look at it together and see what we could make of it. Three or four lines of Rose's typescript have been scribbled out efficiently by Hamilton Johnson with a heavy black pen, the marks like a roll of thick wire over the typed letters. Just here or there he's missed the downward stroke of a 'p', the tail of a 'g', and we manage to piece together a few words: '… when I tried to give him up … beginning …' We hold it up to the desklamp but then the typed letters on the reverse of the page show through, further obscuring the words inked out by Johnson. I'd be ready to swear that Rose is giving him no biography-changing revelation; I'm sure she's talking about the state of her soul.

In my own bundle I discover that Constance has deleted some of Rose's references to other writers: Somerset Maugham's name removed from a discussion of 'ruthless' novelists who put other people's secret love affairs into their novels; 'very autobiographical, I believe' removed from a description of Graham Greene's *The Heart of the Matter*. She has also cut out the names of some (but not all) of the priests Rose has seen preaching at the various local Anglican churches she is currently trying out for suitability, now that she has been absolved by Hamilton Johnson and is back in a relationship with her God. A Reverend Whiteman has been cut from her visit to Grosvenor Chapel, along with his sermon which 'had sense and intelligence.'

I can see that the content of some of Constance's cuts might have been deemed libelous if published, but that doesn't explain an embargo, does it? Constance and then her niece Veronica retained rights over these letters (or rather they believed they did); no-one else could have published them in their entirety anyway.

Martin and I had just swapped folders, getting up to stand beside the duty librarian's high desk that overlooks the scholars' table, and formally passing the folders to him and receiving each other's from his hands, when the phone rang. It was the head librarian, from the far end of the library. 'Sorry,' said our man, 'we have to evacuate the library. There's been a bomb scare.'

That was how our week started. Insofar as the librarians at the Wren can hustle a person, they hustled us out, without the coats and bags that we'd obediently deposited in the cupboard behind the desk in the first alcove. Fortunately Martin had his wallet in his jacket pocket, so we were able to go for coffee, thinking that by the time we returned the bomb scare would have been uncovered as a hoax. Four and a half hours later, after the all-clear from an RAF bomb squad, whose bomb-seeking robot had left sinister deep tracks across the perfect lawn of Nevile's Court, we were allowed back in, cold, frustrated, and tired out from the constant can we?, can't we? and tracking to and from the porters' lodge for information.

Father Johnson's second deletion comes in a letter of 12 August 1951, in a paragraph about Kate O'Brien's novel *Mary Lavelle*, and follows a deletion of Constance's in which Rose bemoans O'Brien's 'lamentable lack' of 'artistic sense and taste and moral background'. On this occasion there's nothing written on the reverse of the page and when I hold it up to the magnifying light I manage to make out the typed letters beneath the thick trail of Johnson's ink. Rose claims (not entirely accurately) that in her own novels she has never represented 'such things', that is, unlawful love affairs, in a favourable light: 'because though involved myself for nearly 25 years, I always knew it to be wrong – hence all the turning away from God, who didn't go with it. But my companion (I have told you this before, I think) saw it all almost *as* God – I mean as one of his highest expressions.'

What aspect of this statement did Hamilton Johnson wish to keep hidden? I'd like to think that he was concerned for Gerald O'Donovan's wife and children, who, I imagine, might have been upset to read that their husband/father considered his affair with Rose Macaulay to have been one of God's highest expressions. I suspect, however, that Johnson wanted to cover up Rose's admission that she had turned away from God for twenty-five years; this might have seemed to him (I speculate) more important than protecting the feelings of other people, for whom, on the whole, he shows a fine disregard. One of the least attractive elements of this correspondence is the frequent low-level gossip about the state of other people's sinful souls: not just Rose's friends and acquaintances who are having affairs (names removed by Constance) but parishioners of Hamilton Johnson, whose secrets he has, presumably, heard in the confessional. In the published letter Rose goes on to say that maybe Kate O'Brien's characters, Mary Lavelle and her lover Juanito, see their own affair as God-sanctioned, and that maybe this is how Kate O'Brien sees it too.

Wednesday 13 June

Rose's references to Reverend, or Father, Whiteman, have become more frequent, and, I find, increasingly predictable. I know when he's going to be the subject of an omission before I check in the manuscript letter. When Rose writes about Grosvenor Chapel, now her favourite place of worship, the ellipses usually concern an eloquent and intelligent sermon preached by Fr Whiteman; if she's writing about a book she's been reading, then any ellipses cover the fact she's going to lend it (or has lent it) to Fr Whiteman, his opinion of it, or the discussion she's had with him about it; if she writes about being ill with undulant fever, as she often is (and, being bedridden, unable to type, so these letters are especially indecipherable), then any ellipsis, sure as night follows day, will cover whether or not, when and how, Fr Whiteman will be bringing her the 'Reserved Sacrament'. Sometimes just his name is omitted, sometimes whole paragraphs are represented by Constance's three dots. Martin has suggested we order photocopies of any chunks that are longer than a few lines, to save us pencilling them (pens are forbidden at the scholars' table) into our own copies of *Letters* and *Last Letters*. If I were here on my own, I don't think I'd bother. I've already taken to scribbling against the ellipses: Father W, blah blah. When I reported this to Martin as we set off to get our lunchtime sandwiches, he said, 'I'm scandalised!' And I think he was, too. Over coffee in the Michaelhouse café Martin told me that on Monday night he dreamed that he was waiting for the sealed box to be opened, with a special list of things to look out for, but when he awoke he couldn't recall what they were. In return for such a confidence I told him about this journal, my *Dreaming of Rose*. Apart from one ill-remembered dream about visiting a Rose Macaulay theme park, I haven't dreamt about her for months. Perhaps I should hand over to Martin oneiric responsibility for Rose?

Rose – in this afternoon's reading – continues now and again to visit other churches, and gossips to Father Johnson about the priests she meets, how high or low they stand, which ones are serious and intelligent, how none of them measure up to Father Whiteman. He and Johnson are her two Prophets, she tells him, her two wise guides; how fortunate she is to have them! It's as if Rose is desperate to be a part of this Boys' Own club. In her old age she yearns to join the clergy, just as in her youth she yearned to join the navy, until her father brutally told her it was impossible for a girl. Those childhood issues – including her father-love – were never resolved. Did she fall in love with Gerald O'Donovan *because* he was (or had been) a priest?

By now we're on to the second volume of letters, which begin in September 1952. Rose is off to join the Retreat of a select band of Anglicans calling themselves the Company of the Way, led by Father Whiteman. What Father Whiteman thinks about Hell, what Father Whiteman thinks about the fear of death, what he thinks about this, what he thinks about that. I'm beginning to feel increasingly fed up with Father Whiteman. My impatience is contagious; Martin, still ahead of me chronologically, leans over the table and whispers loudly that I'll be pleased to hear that Father Whiteman is about to go off on a long holiday to recover from the stresses and strains of looking after his London flock. We agree that that will be a huge relief. But before that happens he's hospitalised with shingles. Rose sends bulletins on his state of recovery, on changing estimates of the date of his return to work, along with unflattering comments about the priests who are standing in for him at Grosvenor Chapel. None of them, it seems, is quite as intelligent or sensitive as Father Whiteman. No-one has such a good reading voice. Like someone newly in love, unable to stop herself dropping the name of her beloved into every second sentence, Rose misses no opportunity to mention Father Whiteman. Perhaps a more accurate analogy would be provided by the relationship between an analysand and her psychoanalyst (Rose would turn in her grave, I fear), because it's not, and could never be, on equal terms: while Whiteman is privy to the secrets of her soul (and hears them once a month in confession), she's not privy to his, despite all the daily chat about religious literature, church history, and the finer points of translation from the classics. On 4 August 1954 Rose tells Hamilton Johnson she's just discovered that the poet Alice Meynell had loved 'a priest of her own persuasion' (ie Roman Catholic) 'so much that his superiors had to move him elsewhere.' Without a trace of self-irony she goes on, 'What a lot of priest-devotion there must always have been!' Constance allowed this passage to pass (Alice Meynell had been dead for years), but cut out the following sentences: 'Father Whiteman has this trouble with an American woman who spends the summer in England and in the Chapel. She is a little mad, actually.'

I had thought that if anything was going to be revealed in the embargoed excerpts of these letters it would be about Gerald O'Donovan but, literary gossip aside, they're all about Father Whiteman.

❧

Thursday 14 June

Dr Lara Feigel joined us this morning. She's rather beautiful, with curly dark hair and sky-blue eyes, and so slender it's hard to believe she's the mother of a six-month-old baby. She was wearing a black corduroy knee-length skirt over black tights, a soft jumper whose colour matched the blue of her eyes, and a smart tailored jacket in deep orange, with a large blue and orange brooch sparkling on the lapel. Yesterday at different times two other readers – both of them looking at illuminated manuscript books – shared the scholars' table with us, but today the three of us were alone. Lara, whose fingers fly over the keyboard of her notepad like spiders on speed, offered to type up any excerpts we wanted, but we said we were OK with our system of pencilled notes and photocopy requests, so she started at the beginning of the correspondence typing up the deleted references to the authors in whom she has an interest.

The three of us started in an orderly fashion, each with our paper folder of twenty or so letters. Lara sat next to Martin on one side of the table, while I took a seat opposite. Every so often Lara would consult Martin over a handwritten squiggle, or I would lean over the table and whisper (loudly, as Martin's a bit hard of hearing) about this or that, under the tolerant eye of the duty librarian at his high desk. If I came across a Graham Greene reference for Lara, or something I wanted to show Martin, I'd get up and carry the letter to the other side of the table past the feet of Lord Byron, who sits with an open copy of Childe Harold in one hand and a meditative pencil to chin in the other. Today Martin insisted, now that we're comfortably established as colleagues rather than as rivals, that I have first go chronologically, so I was first to follow the continuing story of the American woman who was so bewitched by Father Whiteman. After failing to extract from him the address for the retreat he was about to lead (for the shadowy Company of the Way that Rose, by now, has joined as a novice, or 'Wayfarer') she stalked him to the train station and then climbed into his compartment after him. 'She has annoyed Father Whiteman to desperation,' writes Rose.

When finally Father Whiteman escapes for his rest and recuperation in a remote farmhouse in Wales, the woman tracks him down and batters on the cottage door 'like a criminal fleeing from justice'. Father Whiteman, 'trembling with rage' – Rose's quote marks, so this is how he must have reported it to her – demands that she leave him alone.

Why did Father Whiteman ask Constance to remove all references to him from the letters? Did he share (with a number of others) the belief that what Rose wrote to her priest in America deserved the confidentiality of the confessional, and therefore should not be made public at all? Or did he baulk at the extravagant praise Rose heaps upon him, the egregious comparisons she makes between him and his fellow-clergy, and the stories she tells of him being pursued by women?

Then we hear that Father Whiteman won't be returning to his pastoral work in London. He appears to have had some kind of breakdown. Rose passes on to Hamilton Johnson the details of Father Whiteman's 'studious regime': he's reading French mystics, writing, meditating, doing a little gardening. She reports how he is missed at Grosvenor Chapel: 'but one must set one's teeth & pursue one's impeded way with resolution.' Alas, his replacement, although quite pleasant, 'lacks thought'. A few months pass – the exchange of letters between Rose and Johnson is less frequent than previously – and Rose reports that Father Whiteman – still in Wales – has told her that the doubts he has struggled with for many years have crystallised. He has lost his faith: he must give up his Orders.

And now I feel a pang of pity for him. No more lunches with Rose Macaulay or John Betjeman or other well-connected members of his congregation, no more discussion of classical texts or Catholic philosophers. Of course he can continue in such pursuits, but not as his tenured work. He has to seek work elsewhere – carpentry is mentioned, as well as book reviewing – and he'll have to find somewhere else to live. But it's not so much the change in his daily circumstances that tugs at my heartstrings, as the fact that Rose, after a mere two or three months of moaning to Hamilton Johnson about how bereft she feels, has already found someone else. Grosvenor Chapel having lost its magic, Rose has transferred her loyalties (with Hamilton Johnson's blessing) to St Paul's, Knightsbridge (where Princess Margaret, a fan of *The Towers of Trebizond*, sometimes worships) and its incumbent, Father Henderson, 'a priest of great spiritual life and power' who, like Father Whiteman, has the gift of 'perfect enunciation'.

At lunchtime I sat with Lara and Martin on the low wall outside King's while we ate our sandwiches, with French students chattering like starlings on either side of us and herds of Japanese tourists clicking past us along the pavement. We'd reached the last few letters, and Martin had already ordered up a box of correspondence from Trinity's Trevelyan archive that he wanted to look at for another research project. Lara was going to look at any correspondence there might be in the other Macaulay boxes between Constance and Graham Greene or any of the other writers she's working on. She had also ordered up from a different box the one and only photograph of the adult Rose held in the archive. When I was working on my biography I looked at everything in the other boxes of Macaulay/Babington Smith material, but that was a long time ago and I can't remember if I saw any correspondence between Constance and Father Whiteman. Why should I remember? His name would have meant nothing to me.

Rose kept the true nature of her relationship with Gerald O'Donovan a secret from all but a few close friends for twenty-five years or more; Constance, by excising Father Whiteman from Rose's letters and then embargoing the excised material, kept secret Rose's relationship with *him* for twice that long. Not that I believe for a moment that Rose felt anything other than what was entirely proper (if somewhat over the top) for Father Whiteman, but I'm reminded of what Jenny Newman scribbled on this manuscript when I asked her to read an earlier draft. Alongside my description of the Daily Mail headline, DID THIS PRIEST BETRAY THIS WOMAN?, that stoked the controversy over Constance's publication of the correspondence, Jenny wrote: 'Goodness – RM and her 'priests'!'

When we returned to the Wren we found two of the librarians looking unhappily at what had become a high wall of boxes on the trolley. Our yellow order slips lay heaped like autumn leaves on the High Desk. Martin, with what I considered a bold disregard for the librarians' palpable anxiety (or was it just that he hadn't caught their uneasy whispers?), said that he would like, before moving on to the Trevelyan archive, to have another go at trying to decipher the two sections of the letters – quite early letters – inked out by Hamilton Johnson. This necessitated the moving of some of the new boxes over to a table in the alcove and the rearrangement of others from off the trolley and onto the edge of the High Desk. I heard the senior librarian mutter: 'I've never known such chaos.' Meanwhile the photograph ordered by Lara, which had been extracted from its box in the basement and sent upstairs – according to the junior librarian in a louder, more panicked tone than the Wren is accustomed to – was nowhere to be seen.

The Macaulay catalogue shows four letters from Harry Whiteman to Constance: two in box 10, one in box 13, and one in box 14. The two in box 10 are dated early 1963: in one Whiteman describes the long hours of work he's obliged to put in as librarian at the Royal Automobile Club in Pall Mall; in the other he says he's had to move house, and has found a 'rather noble bed-sitter' in the Brompton Road. 'Very pleasant, clean house, housing old oddities like me.' The only problem is the roar of traffic.

Lara offers to type up copies of these letters as Martin has moved on to his Trevelyan material, and our photocopying list is now full. 'Poor old Father Whiteman,' I say as I hand them across the table.

Box 13 yields a courteous letter of thanks from Whiteman to Constance, dated 26 October 1961, for the copy of *Letters to a Friend* she's sent him. He starts his third paragraph: 'I still regard Fr Johnson's decision to publish with mixed feelings, particularly in view of Rose's expectation that the letters would find their way to the incinerator.' He hopes that 'the controversies aroused by publication' haven't proved 'too troublesome' for her, and praises the way she's handled the material.

When I read his fourth letter to Constance, I gasp out loud. Written almost exactly a year later, Whiteman is thanking Constance for the second volume of letters, and telling her that as a result of the quality of her work on them he has 'progressively abdicated' from his first doubts about their publication. How especially nice it is, he writes, to include photographs. And then: 'The frontispiece was taken when I was with Rose in Venice and all of them are very much as I remember her, and lovely to have.' In my amazement I call out to Lara and Martin: Look, Father Whiteman was in Venice with Rose. 'When?' asks Martin: 'Rose took two trips to Venice in her last years.' The caption to the frontispiece, which shows Rose slender in a print silk frock and silk hat, perched on some ancient piece of Venetian stone, possibly a baptismal font, carved with acanthus leaves and capering beasts, says: 'photographed by Roloff Beny in 1957.' 'Ah,' says Martin, 'I think that was the trip she took with Bishop Henderson and his wife.' At that moment the duty librarian finds, at last, on the table in the alcove that houses the catalogues, the photograph that Lara had requested, and brings it over to her. It is the very same photo. Now as I look at it I imagine people standing just out of shot, on either side of the deceptively solitary-looking Rose: Father (now Bishop) Henderson, Father (now Harry) Whiteman, and who knows how many other priests?

I feel a wild laughter rising inside me. Enough! Enough of secrets and embargoes, enough of whether or not these letters should have been published, and whether or not Constance had the legal right to decide about them anyway. Enough of it all! It's time for me to say goodbye to Rose and her priests, and also to sweet-faced Constance, who incurred

14. Rose Macaulay photographed in Venice in 1957, with no priests visible. Roloff Beny.

disapproval from all sides – O'Donovans, Babingtons and Smiths; Anglicans, Roman Catholics and plain old agnostics – for publishing the letters, and whom for years I've loved to imagine at the garden party she once described to Rose, surrounded by heavily-bearded Orthodox priests, in her pearl necklace, and wearing her eccentric bomber-shaped home-made hat.

Epilogue: About the *Letters*

Reconstructing anyone's life poses enormous difficulties, for however copious the evidence of letters, diaries, journals, and eye-witness accounts, the problem of interpretation remains, the problem of the subjectivity of witnesses, and of the basic contradictoriness of the human being. Moods and emotions are volatile, but when recorded on the page are often forced by posterity to carry a much greater weight than was ever intended by their author. In her book on E M Forster, Rose Macaulay criticised his unsympathetic response to a letter of Jane Austen's. Jane Austen wrote to her sister Cassandra: 'Mrs Hall was brought to bed yesterday of a dead child, some weeks before she expected, owing to a fright. I suppose she happened unawares to look at her husband.' Forster disliked the unkindness of this, and imagined Jane and Cassandra laughing together over unfortunate Mrs Hall and her ugly husband. But Cassandra's reaction might have been very different, Rose pointed out. She might have chided Jane for unkindness. Jane might have repented. We can never know. 'That is the worst of publishing the letters of the dead,' concluded Rose. 'They grin and stare and grimace and scowl at us, expressing for ever, in black ink on paper, moods which were scarcely even moods, so glibly did they run by, run off the pen' (Macaulay 1938, 251).

When *Letters to a Friend*, the first volume of Rose Macaulay's letters to Father Hamilton Johnson, was published in October 1961, the revelations it contained about her love affair with a married man provoked from critics and from the general public a wide range of passionate reactions. The publication also started a controversy in the press over the ethics of publishing private letters. The *Daily Mail* quoted Rebecca West, who said, 'It made me want to vomit' (Churchill, 12 October 1961); on the other side the Archbishop of Canterbury, choosing a rather more episcopalian mode of diction, pronounced: 'I cannot but think that good will come of the book' (ERM 13).

The arguments fell into two broad groups. First, the biographical argument: what were, or, depending on one's interpretation, what would have been, the wishes of the author, Rose Macaulay, regarding the publication of the letters? And what weight should be given to those expressed or imputed wishes? Secondly, the religious or ethical argument over the content of the letters: that is, Rose Macaulay's admission of adultery, her expressions of remorse, and her return to the Church. But the two arguments become inextricably entangled in the double question of what right, if any, and what need, if any, the public had to read the letters.

The huge fuss over the contents of the letters seems curiously dated. It is hard to imagine now the sense of sin which was then, in the early 1960s, a part of many people's consciousness. Since then Britain has become a largely secular society; Rose's expressions of remorse for her sin carry a historical rather than a topical interest for the reader.

The letters were made public in a world which would soon be very different from the one in which they had been written. Already there were indications of things loosening up: in 1960 *Lady Chatterley's Lover* had been unbanned in the courts; in 1961 the contraceptive pill went on sale in Britain for the first time. By 1965, the year a woman was first appointed to be a High Court judge, an opinion poll revealed that although the majority of people in Britain still believed in God, most of them would rather watch television than go to church.

Yet the questions raised by the arguments over the private versus the public ownership of letters, diaries and journals are enduring in relation to the work of biography. How do we know what the subject would have wished? If there were written instructions, as there were in the case of Rose Macaulay's letters to Hamilton Johnson, how do we interpret those instructions? Even if we do know what the subject wished, is the biographer's duty to the subject, or to posterity?

These questions were raised by the publication of the two volumes of *Letters* in 1961 and 1962; and raised again when, in 1964, a third volume of letters came out, those of Rose to her younger sister Jean (*Letters to a Sister*, 1964). All three volumes were edited by Constance Babington Smith.

Rose had met Constance Babington Smith, a distant cousin, in the 1950s at St Paul's in Knightsbridge, which Rose sometimes attended instead of Grosvenor Chapel.

When Rose died in October 1958, Constance had not met Jean Macaulay, but soon after their first meeting a friendship began to grow that had its roots in their shared Christian beliefs and practices

15. Constance Babington Smith, at the time the *Letters* were published.
   Gerry Bauer.

and in their devotion to the memory of Rose. Later, after Jean's lifelong companion Nancy Willetts had died, Constance became Jean's closest friend and carer and the two women would regularly attend church retreats together. Meanwhile Jean, probably because she felt she lacked the necessary literary knowledge and sophistication, had transferred to Constance control of the copyright in all her sister's unpublished work.

On her death Rose Macaulay had left instructions that all the papers in her flat should be burned unread (Rose Macaulay to Jean Macaulay, 13 August 1956, ERM Box 9). This was used to support the argument by those opposed to the publication of the Hamilton Johnson letters that letters *from* Rose should also be destroyed. Constance and Jean disputed the logic of this argument; they went further, and maintained that the reason that Rose had asked for all the papers in her flat to be destroyed was to ensure that one particular cousin, a convert to Roman Catholicism, should not be able to go through them. Of all Rose's prejudices her prejudice against Roman Catholics in her latter years was one of the liveliest. Her opinion of that branch of Christianity had not changed since she wrote of it that 'it will save you a lot of trouble in deciding for yourself what to believe, for it knows the truth and tells you' (Macaulay 1925, 7). It is not impossible that she said something to Jean or Constance about her fear of this cousin going through her private papers after her death.

In the story of the publication of these letters, much hinges on the interpretation of remarks. On the one hand a remark about a Roman Catholic cousin which was not backed up by written evidence was used by Constance and Jean as a guide to Rose's intentions; on the other hand a quite specific request, in writing, to the recipient of her letters that he burn them all, was dismissed by Constance and Jean as a casual remark. Rose had written to Father Hamilton Johnson on 7 September 1952: 'I'm *glad* you like to have my letters. Really 100? I think you'd better get rid of them, of any you have kept, in that incinerator! I own I have kept yours – but that is another matter. They are full of such good stuff – how good you have been to me these 2 years! But I will burn them before I die; they're not for other people to see. How I value all that liturgical world you have opened to me' (Macaulay 1961, 358). Constance called Rose's reference to the incinerator 'flippant' (perhaps, although Constance didn't say this, because of the exclamation mark, perennially an unreliable indicator of tone). As Rose was not dismayed when she discovered later that Hamilton Johnson had ignored the instruction, Constance said, it indicated that she hadn't meant it seriously.

In a review of the first volume of the *Letters* in the *Spectator*, Stevie Smith pointed out some of the inconsistencies in the demands Rose made of Hamilton Johnson, giving as an example the way Rose would tell Hamilton Johnson in one letter not to bother to read one of her books, and in the next letter want to know exactly what he thought of it. Stevie Smith, a careful reader, said, 'it makes one wonder if, when she says, "Put these letters in your incinerator," she means it' (Smith 1961). Rose's close friend the literary and music critic Raymond Mortimer expressed even stronger doubts over Rose's desire to have her letters destroyed, and did not even address the incinerator question: 'She loved to read books of good letters,' he wrote in the *Sunday Times*, 'and I think must have guessed that her own would be published, if she left no instructions to the contrary, which she never did' (Mortimer 1961). He believed that because Rose herself was a writer, there was a duty to posterity to publish letters with a bearing on that writing career. How can we understand writers, goes his argument, if we know nothing of what moves them deeply, in this case Rose's profound feelings of alienation and exile, her yearning to re-enter the Church of her youth, a love affair that lasted almost a quarter century, and the 'supreme importance' of her devotional life in her last eight years?

By the time the first volume was published Father Hamilton Johnson, too, was dead. He and Constance Babington Smith had met in 1956 when she travelled to America and, with an introductory letter from Rose, had visited him at the Cowley Fathers Monastery in Boston. He had sent to Constance all the letters he had received from Rose. Or not quite all: there is a mysterious missing page, 'missing when the correspondence was received', according to Constance, from Rose's fourth letter to him, dated 27 November 1950, a crucial period two months before she took the plunge and, for the first time in 30 years, went to confession (Macaulay 1961, 35). For Constance it was important that the publication of the letters should have received Hamilton Johnson's blessing but others felt that his views, being those of the recipient rather than the author of the letters, were not relevant; they remained unimpressed when Constance made public his expressed wish that the letters should be published 'as they might be of help to many' (Macaulay 1961, 7). Some felt that not only were his views irrelevant, but that by handing over the letters for publication he had betrayed the trust Rose had placed in him.

E M Forster was among those who felt that way. After he had read the extracts published in the *Observer* he wrote to Constance Babington Smith that he was surprised not to have seen a statement announcing that the letters were being published by Rose's own expressed wish (ERM, Box 13). He presumed there would be such a statement in the book. Of course there was no such statement, and none of Constance's considerable mollifying skills had any effect on his implacable hostility to the publication. E M Forster had a personal stake in upholding the privacy of personal letters, for sexual revelations could brand people as criminals (male homosexuality was a criminal offence until the Sexual Offences Act of 1967). But that was only one factor, and one that was not paralleled in Rose's letters to Hamilton Johnson, for Rose admitted to no crime, only to a 'sin'; the equivalent risk for a woman (lesbianism was never a criminal offence) would have been the revelation of having procured an abortion. But Forster's hostility to the enterprise was grounded in a more general cultural position. Like Rose herself, he was part of a culture that valued restraint and reticence; intimate gossip among close friends was one thing, but the publication of such intimacies was beyond the pale. He may well also have felt, as did other humanist and secular friends of Rose, a distaste for the intrusive religiosity of the correspondence. Some indeed felt a strong animosity towards Hamilton Johnson; Elizabeth Bowen referred to him as 'that rat-faced priest' (quoted in Wilson 1992, 147) and V S Pritchett, in the *New Statesman*, called him 'the dog-collared fan', who wasted too much of a busy writer's time in the last years of her life (Pritchett 1964).

Constance was astonished by the controversy that surrounded the publication of *Letters to a Friend*. It is surely a measure of her innocence in the matter that she had chosen to end the first volume with the letter in which Rose had so specifically talked about the destruction of her letters in an incinerator. And it is perhaps a measure of the canniness of Viola Garvin, literary editor of the *Observer*, that she chose to end the first week's selected extracts from the book with that letter. No wonder it drew attention.

If you read the correspondence surrounding the publication of the letters it is hard to question Constance Babington Smith's honesty and good faith. She saw the story of Rose's return to the Church, as told in the *Letters*, as a triumphant conclusion to the story that was begun but left unfinished in Rose's last published novel, *The Towers of Trebizond*. But her interpretation was only one of many, and the question of how to read the letters was taken out of her hands as soon as the first volume of them was published.

On publication the letters no longer belonged just to the editor, Constance Babington Smith, nor to the late recipient, nor to the writer's surviving relatives, nor, even, to the presumed constituency of the book's readership, those wavering Christians and agnostics whom Constance addressed in her introduction and her prefatory remarks. The serialisation of the book over two Sundays (8 October and 15 October) in the *Observer*, and the full-page article in the *Daily Mail* (12 October), with its headline 'Did this priest betray this woman?', illustrated with a full-face picture of Rose Macaulay wearing a dark beret and looking – despite the fact that she was the one 'betrayed' rather than the one 'betraying' – like a Russian spy, ensured a much wider and more vociferous expression of opinion than Constance had dreamed of. In the next few months Constance and Jean – in their innocence – consoled each other with the thought that at least more people would read the book, and that when they did read it they would respond to its uplifting moral message.

In the first week of the *Observer* extracts, adultery was highlighted at the expense of liturgy, and in the second week of serialisation Rose's not altogether complimentary comments about Graham Greene were singled out and printed around a large photograph of him. Rhona Churchill drew attention in the *Daily Mail* to Constance's control of the copyright and suggested, to the horror and distress of both Constance and Jean, that she had published the letters for her own financial gain. It was Rhona Churchill who elicited from Rebecca West that the publication of the book made her 'want to vomit' (Churchill, 12 October 1961). This provoked Raymond Mortimer, in turn, into suggesting that Dame Rebecca West was 'not well-balanced' and because of her own past, was 'specially fussed about sexual irregularity' (Mortimer, 22 October 1961). There were a number of other accusations like this: one correspondent in the *Observer* said that 'adulterers and adulteresses' had been 'touched on the raw' and that publication of the letters provided a posthumous recompense for the sin that in life Rose Macaulay had not been able to rectify (Anon, 15 October 1961).

Two or three weeks after publication, when emotions were running at their highest and Constance was under attack from all sides, her brother wrote her a letter of stout support: he thought that the purpose of the book was 'to show how a great personality wrestled with temptation and sin and triumphed over it' (ERM, Box 13). This is a fine example of what many people wanted the book to show, rather than what it actually did show. For, as we have seen, the *Letters* do not chart a Dantean descent into hell; they articulate barely a nodding acquaintance with temptation and sin, let alone a wrestling with it. For much of the *Letters* Rose seems to be seeking, and thanking Father Johnson for providing, reassurance that her own type of faith, or belief, or hope, was sufficient to allow her a place within the Church. 'An active Christian,' William Plomer described her in his review of the third volume, *Letters to a Sister*, 'she may also be called an elastic one' (Plomer 1964). In the three volumes of letters a wide-ranging interest in Christianity is displayed; but there is truth in the criticism made by Marghanita Laski in the *Observer* that 'too much is churchiness rather than religion' (Laski, 14 October 1962).

And as for the nature of the sin, that too was widely interpreted. Stevie Smith drew a distinction between sinfulness and guilt, saying that in the book there was 'no sinfulness of serious sort, though she (Rose) makes much of her feelings of guilt for an old love affair' (Smith, 27 October 1961). Some correspondents maintained that there had been no sin at all; others expressed their unease at the sight of a woman of Rose Macaulay's experience and sophistication turning to a celibate man for guidance on the troubles of her sexual life.

The lack of profound spiritual or religious matter in the letters did not, however, stop Christian readers from taking passionate sides. Although in the introduction to the first volume Constance quoted a lengthy passage from a letter she had received from Hamilton Johnson in which he insisted that Rose had made no confession to him (he confused the issue by stating that it was 'as if' he had been a priest in a confessional-box listening to 'her situation'; Macaulay 1961, 23), a number of people nonetheless read the letters as a betrayal not just of the trust invested in a friendship, but of the seal of the confessional. Against those people, at the other extreme, were ranged the correspondents who believed that Rose had only *thought* she was confessing but had been sadly mistaken; Hamilton Johnson, they maintained, being an Anglican, was no priest at all; he was one of those men 'calling themselves priests' and 'dressing up' as priests, a fake with no spiritual authority. (Box 13 in the Emilie Rose Macaulay archive contains a range of responses, including this and the following one, received by Constance in the weeks following the publication of *Letters to a Friend*.)

Nor was comment of a personal nature lacking from the inter-Christian contingent. Whereas both the broad-based Roman Catholic *Tablet* and the Dominican *Blackfriars* gave the book good reviews -- which greatly pleased Constance and led her to express the hope, a pious hope if ever there was one, that this indicated a 'thaw' in RC/Anglican relations – it was reviewed rudely in the Anglican journal *Theology*. It was a dean who reviewed it. In no time at all he was being described as having 'only a third-class degree' and writing for an editor who was notorious for having recently 'turned queer' on a number of other issues.

The secular responses – leaving aside Rebecca West who may well have regretted what she had said once she saw it in the *Daily Mail* – included those who agreed with E M Forster's opinion that without Rose Macaulay's stated wish for publication no one had any business to publish the letters. Others, including Raymond Mortimer, Harold Nicolson and William Plomer, welcomed publication for the picture the letters gave of Rose's varied interests, her intellectual curiosity, her sharpness (Raymond Mortimer's only criticism was of her obsession with the faults of Roman Catholics) and, in general, her love of life. Harold Nicolson found the letters 'charming and gay', and praised them for enhancing the zest of pagans like himself (Nicolson, 22 October 1961). William Plomer wrote of how Rose's 'love of travel, of history, of literature and of persons coursed through her old veins and courses through these pages' (Plomer, 26 October 1961). Raymond

Mortimer felt that he was 'once again listening to her deliciously pointed talk' (Mortimer, 22 October 1961). What these three men read into the letters was a confirmation of Rose's happiness in the last eight years of her life, and as good friends of hers they could not but be happy on her behalf. 'Her joyous faith halved all her worries and doubled all her joys,' wrote pagan Harold Nicolson with generosity (Nicolson, 22 October 1961).

All three of these writers praised Constance's editing. Harold Nicolson said she brought to the task 'a charming modesty, coupled with that intense gift of perception which enabled her to detect the V.2 (sic) at Peenemünde before it was launched, thus saving many thousands from destruction' (Nicolson, 22 October 1961).

It is as if, for her friends, reading the *Letters* brought Rose back to them. The subjectivity of their response is obvious; it is as if they can hear Rose speaking. For those who didn't know Rose so well, it was a little different, but for them too the response was subjective. Perhaps letters particularly bring out that response in readers; they are, after all, addressed to an individual 'you'. It is hard not to become, at least partly, that 'you' when you are reading.

Some people detected in the *Letters* an expression of the loneliness of old age, including two of those who wrote most perspicaciously about them, V S Pritchett and Marghanita Laski. Laski challenged Hamilton Johnson's statement that the letters could be 'of help to many'. 'But whom are the letters to help?' she asked, in her review of the second volume in October 1962. 'It is no help to know that in old age, in loss and loneliness, many people turn or return to the Church, for gladly or sadly, according to our bias, we knew this already'. And like others who were not sympathetic to what they read, she disliked Constance's 'assiduous annotations' (Laski, 14 October 1962). Pritchett wrote of Rose Macaulay's 'touching attempt to break out of loneliness', and expressed sorrow at the 'very familiar sight' of someone feeling guilt and being induced to believe that the anguish and pain she had suffered was all due to a 'sin' (Pritchett 1964).

But amongst all the letters and articles carefully preserved by Constance Babington Smith, that show such a range of sympathy and antipathy, that are so revealing about the beliefs and hopes and anxieties of their writers, there is one gaping hole. No one admits to the hurt they felt when they discovered the secret that had been kept from them. Rose Macaulay loved someone in successful secrecy for a quarter of a century and hid her grief at his loss for years afterwards. How could friends and acquaintances not have been hurt by that revelation? And how could they not be further hurt when they read Raymond Mortimer saying, inaccurately, that 'the long, reciprocated love of Rose Macaulay for a married man was a fact known to a large circle' (Mortimer, 22 October 1961) if they had counted themselves as Rose's friends, but were not, somehow, part of this 'large circle'?

Rose's fellow-writers may have been divided over the ethics of publishing the letters, but on the whole they agreed that their contents failed to show Rose Macaulay's strengths as a writer. Stevie Smith worried that the 'dangerous charm' of the inconsequentiality of the author's voice left a 'smear of triviality' over the subjects discussed (Smith 1961). Marghanita Laski found a 'cloying flavour of over-enthusiastic self-indulgence' in the apparent lack of spiritual austerity, self-discipline and self-sacrifice (Laski, 14 October 1962). V S Pritchett, while being one of those who imagined that Rose Macaulay would have been dismayed by the exploitation of her privacy, still found what he called a 'lop-sided' biographical value in the two volumes. 'They reveal a decorous mind that must be set beside the mind of the satirist and the rebel in her, which produced her best work' (Pritchett 1964). While certain facts about Rose Macaulay's life – the love affair, her commitment to the Church – may have come as news to readers, Pritchett was one of only a few to find himself moved to a reappraisal. For most, it was the Rose they already knew who was in the letters; or it was the Rose they already knew who had been betrayed by the publication of the letters.

So it was that the notorious Macaulay reticence became part of the weaponry in the argument over publication. Throughout her life Rose Macaulay had guarded and cherished her sense of privacy. In 1934 she was pleading with an American anthologist to remove her biographical details from his book. Later she replied angrily to a request from a researcher for *Who's Who* that it was neither coyness nor affectation that motivated her desire to deny him personal details. She wrote a novel on the subject, *I Would be Private* (1937). E M Forster was accurate in his assessment of her as reticent like himself; and Rebecca West was right to talk of Rose's dignity and fastidiousness. But there were other Roses. There was Raymond Mortimer's Rose, who could be 'cavalier in her treatment of facts' (ERM archive, Box 13); there was James Lees-Milne's Rose, who was 'unworldly, indiscreet, impulsive, but intensely lovable as well as very clever indeed' (Lees-Milne 1964, 287). There was even the Rose of Malcolm Muggeridge's splendidly eccentric vision, a Rose 'so earnest, so clever, so wrong!' that he imagines her as 'the final destroyer of the human race' (Muggeridge, 14 April 1964).

Each reader of the *Letters* brought their own Rose to their reading; just as, finally, each biographer brings their own subject to the biography. Constance's Rose, in her edition of the *Letters*, was not, is not, and could never be, the Rose of other readers.

When the first fuss had died down, and when, a year later, Constance and Jean had weathered the publication of *Last Letters to a Friend* (which contained no further private revelations), they remained committed to their view that the books would help people and would have far-reaching effects on their moral lives. By then they had received numerous letters from Christian readers that vindicated this view. Their devotion both to the Christian Church and to the memory of Rose Macaulay is unquestionable. What Rose herself would have thought we can only speculate, as so many did on publication. It is hard not to think that she would have been a bit impatient with all the religious fan letters that so pleased her sister and her cousin. After the second volume came out Marjorie Grant Cook, who perhaps more than anyone was privy to the secrets of Rose's heart, wrote to Constance: 'I am now sure that Rose would have said, "Yes, publish after my death". And that for mixed reasons, not really missionary' (ERM Box 13). Marjorie Grant Cook was doubtless right about the mixed reasons: one of those would surely have been for the sheer pleasure in provoking such argument and controversy. Another might well have been to see the vindication of Rose's long-held views – explored first in *Potterism*, the novel that made her a household name in 1920 – on the power and the perniciousness of the press.

What value do the letters have now? Any editor publishing letters soon after the death of the writer, and any biographer writing about a recently dead subject, is faced with decisions about what to leave out. A subject's desire for privacy, expressed or inferred, then becomes less important than the responsibility not to cause hurt or offence to living people and indeed not to lay oneself and one's publisher open to charges of libel or slander. Paradoxically, the further away in time you are from the subject, the more you are able to know about the people they moved among.

The intactness of what is published depends on whose hands the letters have passed through. Rose Macaulay's letters to her sister Jean were extensively edited by Jean before Constance began her own editorial process.

But Constance has left for public access the correspondence she had with people featured in all three volumes of the *Letters*, and it is often more revealing than what appeared in the final version. Constance was scrupulous in contacting everyone who might conceivably have been offended by Rose's comments on them. Most, but not all, felt that it was more important to have Rose's comments, however biased, appear in print than to delete them.

Graham Greene was one of these, writing to Mark Bonham Carter at Collins that it was better that 'Rose's sweet inaccuracies' about himself should not be edited out (ERM Box 13). Greene being not only a novelist who was then at a particularly prolific period of his career, but also a Roman Catholic convert, was a natural target for much of Rose's musings on other writers' follies and the peculiar and quite inexplicable follies of Roman Catholics. On *The End of the Affair* she wrote: 'The people are all rather low types, and not convincing. And the religion in it (such as it is) is brought down to a very trivial plane by two rather absurd miracles at the end, which are supposed to show the heroine's sanctity, though there are no other signs of this ... What a mess his mind must be – nothing in it, scarcely, but religion and sex, and these all mixed up together' (Macaulay 1961, 196). And on being invited to one of his parties she wrote: 'On Tuesday I am bidden to a party at Graham Greene's. Wouldn't it be interesting if at that party I was surrounded by G G characters – evil men, racing touts, false clergymen, drunken priests and with G G in the middle of them talking about Sin ...' (Macaulay 1961, 343).

Inaccuracies whether sweet or not there were: it was a part of Rose Macaulay just as much as her scrupulous scholarly correspondence with others about seventeenth-century manuscript songs or early editions of *Paradise Lost*. Had the letters been published later than they were, they could have included more of the lively pictures of her contemporaries, such as the exchange Rose recorded between herself and William Plomer one weekend in the country when he admitted to her shyly that he had taken to going to church now and again, and Rose replied that so, too, had she. 'What *would* Morgan say if he could hear us?' asked Rose. (Plomer asked Constance to remove this exchange from the second volume of letters. ERM Box 13.)

The passage of time has meant that E M Forster is no longer alive to be hurt, as William Plomer thought he might be, by two friends whispering behind his back. It has also meant that the significance of the role Gerald O'Donovan played in Rose Macaulay's life and work is what concerns readers now, not, as appears in the *Letters*, the bald fact of his existence. With hindsight, knowing much more about Gerald than was known then, one can see how enormously important the relationship was – how could it not have been? – but in the letters his existence appears as not much more than the reason for the regret and remorse that Rose Macaulay was feeling in the decade after his death, and her reason for returning to the Church. The *Letters* no longer seem particularly revelatory. Nor do they tell us a great deal about Rose Macaulay as a writer because that was not what they were primarily about. She was a prolific, but not a great, letter writer. At the time of publication Stevie Smith and Marghanita Laski criticised the letters on literary grounds, and concluded that Rose Macaulay reserved her creative power for her books. That seems to me a fair judgement.

Works by Rose Macaulay

All titles are novels unless otherwise indicated.

Abbots Verney (London: John Murray, 1906).

The Furnace (London: John Murray, 1907).

The Secret River (London: John Murray, 1909).

The Valley Captives (London: John Murray, 1911).

Views and Vagabonds (London: John Murray, 1912).

The Lee Shore (London: Hodder & Stoughton, 1912).

The Two Blind Countries (London: Sidgwick & Jackson, 1914), poems.

The Making of a Bigot (London: Hodder & Stoughton, 1914).

Non-Combatants and Others (London: Hodder & Stoughton, 1916).

What Not: A Prophetic Comedy (London: Constable, 1918).

Three Days (London: Constable, 1919), poems.

Potterism: A Tragi-Farcical Tract (London: Collins, 1920).

Dangerous Ages (London: Collins, 1921).

Mystery at Geneva. An Improbable Tale of Singular Happenings
(London: Collins, 1922).

Told by an Idiot (London: Collins, 1923).

Orphan Island (London: Collins, 1924).

A Casual Commentary (London: Methuen, 1925), anthology.

Crewe Train (London: Collins, 1926).

Catchwords and Claptrap (London: Hogarth Press, 1926), critical study.

Keeping Up Appearances (London: Collins, 1928).

Staying with Relations (London: Collins, 1930).

Some Religious Elements in English Literature (London: Hogarth Press, 1931), critical study.

They Were Defeated (London: Collins, 1932).

Going Abroad (London: Collins, 1934).

Milton (London: Duckworth, 1934), critical study.

The Minor Pleasures of Life (London: Gollancz, 1934), anthology.

Personal Pleasures (London: Gollancz, 1935), essays.

I Would Be Private (London: Collins, 1937).

An Open Letter to a Non-Pacifist (London: Peace Pledge Union, 1937), essay.

The Writings of E M Forster (London: Hogarth Press, 1938), critical study.

And No Man's Wit (London: Collins, 1940).

Life among the English (London: Collins, 1942), essay.

They Went to Portugal (London: Jonathan Cape, 1946), history.

Fabled Shore: From the Pyrenees to Portugal (London: Hamish Hamilton, 1949), history.

The World My Wilderness (London: Collins, 1950).

Pleasure of Ruins (London: Weidenfeld and Nicolson, 1953), history.

The Towers of Trebizond (London: Collins, 1956).

Letters To A Friend, From Rose Macaulay, 1950–1952, ed Constance Babington-Smith (London: Collins, 1961), letters.

Last Letters To A Friend, From Rose Macaulay, 1952–1964, ed Constance Babington-Smith (London: Collins, 1963), letters.

They Went to Portugal Too, L C Taylor (ed.) (London: Carcanet, 1990), history.

Works cited

The Emilie Rose Macaulay archive, Wren Library, Trinity College, Cambridge is referred to as ERM in the text. All the letters and press clippings quoted in the Epilogue can be found in ERM Boxes 4, 9 and 13.

Anon, Letter to the editor, *Observer*, 15 October 1961.

Constance Babington Smith, *Rose Macaulay* (London: Collins, 1972).

Rhona Churchill, 'Did this priest betray this woman?', *Daily Mail*, 12 October 1961.

Victor Gollancz, *Reminiscences of Affection* (New York: Athenaeum, 1968).

Richard Holmes, *Footsteps: Adventures of a Romantic Biographer* (London: Hodder & Stoughton, 1985).

Michael Holroyd, *A Book of Secrets: Illegitimate Daughters, Absent Fathers* (London: Chatto & Windus, 2010).

Marghanita Laski, 'Retreat into religion', *Observer*, 14 October 1962.

James Lees-Milne, *A Mingled Measure, 1953–72* (London: John Murray, 1964).

Rose Macaulay, 'How to Choose a Religion', in *A Casual Commentary* (London: Methuen, 1925), 5–13.

—, *Keeping Up Appearances* (1928), (London: Pan, 1949).

—, *Last Letters To A Friend, From Rose Macaulay, 1952–1964*, ed Constance Babington-Smith (London: Collins, 1963).

—, *Letters to a Friend, From Rose Macaulay, 1950–1952*, ed Constance Babington-Smith (London: Collins, 1961).

—, 'Miss Anstruther's Letters' (1942), in *Non-Combatants and Others. Writings Against War, 1916–1945* (Bath: Handheld Press, 2019), 273–282.

—, *The Towers of Trebizond* (London: Collins, 1956).

—, *What Not. A Prophetic Comedy* (1918) (Bath, Handheld Press, 2019).

—, 'Whitewash' (1952) in Cynthia Asquith (ed) *The Second Ghost Book*, (London: Pan books, 1956), 69–74.

—, *The Writings of E M Forster* (London: Hogarth Press, 1938).

Raymond Mortimer, 'A return to faith', *Sunday Times*, 22 October 1961.

Malcolm Muggeridge, 'Dear Rose! So earnest! So clever! So wrong!', *Evening Standard*, 14 April 1964.

Harold Nicolson, 'The joyous faith of Rose Macaulay', *Observer*, 22 October 1961.

Nigel Nicolson and Joanne Trautmann (eds), *The Letters of Virginia Woolf, Vol 6, 1934–1941* (New York: Harcourt Press, 1980).

William Plomer, The way back', *Listener*, 26 October 1961.

—, 'Brief reviews', *Sunday Times*, 5 April 1964.

V S Pritchett, 'Euodias and Syntyche', *New Statesman*, 17 April 1964, 608.

Thomas Pynchon, *Gravity's Rainbow* (New York: Viking Press, 1973).

Gwen Raverat, *Period Piece. A Cambridge Childhood* (London, Faber and Faber, 1952).

Stevie Smith, 'Soul of gossip', *The Spectator*, 27 October 1961, 961.

A N Wilson: 'Rose Macaulay' in *Founders and Followers: Literary Lectures given on the occasion of the 150th Anniversary of the Founding of the London Library* (London: Sinclair-Stevenson, 1992), 127–48.

Index

Page numbers in italics refer to images

M

Nichols, Nancy *see also* Lynd, Gaster   90, 109–111, 118, 165–66
Nicolson, Nigel   129, 134
Nicolson, Harold   58, 195–96

O

Observer 37 (*Thin Woman*)   192–94
O'Donovan, Beryl (née Verschoyle)   6–7, 68, 71–72, 77, 132, 141, 143, 145, 167
O'Donovan, Brigid   72–3, 142–46
O'Donovan, Dermod   54, 38, 72–4, 78, 132, 143
O'Donovan, Father Jeremiah *see* Gerald O'Donovan
O'Donovan, Gerald *see also* Roman Catholicism   6–10, 14, 17–18, 27, 34, 42, 50, 52,
    54, 67–68, 70, 71–74, 77, 78, 80, 81, 88, 93, 132, 136, 141–149, *146*, 166–67, 173,
    177, 179–80, 183, 200
        Father Ralph   6, 72, 144, 145, 148
        The Holy Tree   148
        Waiting   81
O'Donovan, Mary   68, 71, 141
O'Donovan, Mary Anne   50, 52, 54, 59, 67–68, 70–75, 77–78, 109, 131–32, 142, 144

P

Papal Encyclical Against Modernism   148
Peace Pledge Union   5
Pearce, Philippa *see also* Great Shelford   22–23, 48–49, 56, 152
Pembroke College, Cambridge   174–75
Penguin archive, University of Bristol   112–13
Plomer, William   118, 153, 194, 195, 200
Powell, Anthony   36, 50
        Temporary Kings   170
Pritchett, V S   192, 196–97
Pullman, Philip
        Tiger in the Well   33
Purser, Sarah *see also* St Brendan's   142
Pynchon, Thomas
        Gravity's Rainbow   118

R

Raverat, Gwen   165
        Period Piece   164–65
reader, reliable   26
Reynolds, Barbara   49–50, 58, 61, 62, 89, 114

What Not

A Prophetic Comedy

by Rose Macaulay

Rose Macaulay

What Not

A Prophetic Comedy

What Not is Rose Macaulay's speculative novel of post-First World War eugenics and newspaper manipulation that influenced Aldous Huxley's *Brave New World*.

Published in 1918, *What Not* was hastily withdrawn due to a number of potentially libellous pages, and was reissued in 1919, but had lost its momentum. Republished in 2019 with the suppressed pages reinstated for the first time, *What Not* is a lost classic of feminist protest at social engineering, and rage at media manipulation.

Kitty Grammont and Nicholas Chester are in love. Kitty is certified as an A for breeding purposes, but politically ambitious Chester has been uncertificated, and may not marry. Kitty wields power as a senior civil servant in the Ministry of Brains, which makes these classifications, but she does not have the freedom to marry who she wants. They ignore the restrictions, and carry on a discreet affair. But it isn't discreet enough for the media: the popular press, determined to smash the brutal regime of the Ministry of Brains, has found out about Kitty and Chester, and scents an opportunity for a scandalous exposure.

Aldous Huxley was a frequent guest at Macaulay's flat while she was writing *What Not*. Fourteen years later, his *Brave New World* borrowed many of Macaulay's ideas for Huxley's own prophetic vision.

The introduction is by Sarah Lonsdale, senior lecturer in journalism at City University London.

'Her writing is stirring, funny, uniquely imaginative. This book should not be forgotten again' — *The Guardian*

'*What Not* is a forgotten gem in a prolific career' — *The Times*

Potterism

A Tragi-Farcical Tract

by Rose Macaulay

Rose Macaulay's 1920 satire on British journalism and the newspaper industry is about the Potter newspaper empire, and the ways in which journalists struggled to balance the truth and what would sell, during the First World War and into the 1920s. When Jane and Johnny Potter are at Oxford they learn to despise their father's popular newspapers, though they still end up working for the family business. But Jane is greedy, and wants more than society will let her have.

Mrs Potter is a well-known romantic novelist, whose cheap novelettes appear in the shop-girls' magazines. She has become unable to distinguish fact from fiction, and her success gives her an unhealthy estimation of her own influence. Arthur Gideon resists the fake news and gushing sentiment peddled by the Potter press, but an unexpected tragedy binds him even closer to their influence.

The Introduction is by Sarah Lonsdale, senior lecturer in journalism at City University London.

Rose Macaulay
Non-Combatants
and Others
Writings Against War, 1916-1945

Non-Combatants and Others
Writings Against War, 1916–1945
by Rose Macaulay

Rose Macaulay was a columnist, reviewer and pioneering critic of BBC radio in its early days. Here all her anti-war writing is collected together in one fascinating and thought-provoking volume.

- *Non-Combatants and Others* (1916) was the first anti-war novel to be published in the UK during the First World War.
- Her witty, furious and despairing journalism for *The Spectator*, *Time and Tide* and *The Listener* from 1936 to 1945 details the rise of fascism and the civilian response to war.
- 'Miss Anstruther's Letters', a short story of the Blitz, relates the devastating loss of a home, and of all a dead lover's letters.

The Introduction is by Jessica Gildersleeve of the University of Southern Queensland. The cover illustration, 'Peace Angel', is by the Norwegian caricaturist Olaf Gulbransson, published in the German satirical magazine *Simplicissimus* in 1917.

Personal Pleasures

Essays on Enjoying Life

by Rose Macaulay

Rose Macaulay

Personal Pleasures

Essays on Enjoying Life

Rose Macaulay was passionately interested in everyday life and its foolishnesses. *Personal Pleasures* is an anthology from 1935 of 80 of her short essays (some of them very short) about the things she enjoyed most in life. Her subjects include:

- Bed (Getting Into It)
- Booksellers' Catalogues
- Christmas Morning
- Driving a Car
- Flattery
- Heresies
- Not Going to Parties
- Shopping Abroad
- Writing

While each essay can be read on its own as a delicious morsel of discerning writing, the collection is also an autobiographical selection, revealing glimpses of Rose's own life, and making us laugh helplessly with her inimitable humour.

The introduction is by Kate Macdonald, editor of *Rose Macaulay, Gender and Modernity* (2018), Visiting Research Fellow at Oxford Brookes University.

To be published in September 2021.

Marjorie Grant

Latchkey
Ladies

Latchkey Ladies

by Marjorie Grant

Latchkey Ladies opens in 1918 in the Mimosa Club, a women's boarding house in central London where young women office workers and ladies on declining incomes take refuge from the tedium of war work and the chilliness of impending poverty. Anne Carey is a secretary, engaged to a young lieutenant in the army, but she is bored of him, bored of poetry and bored of the war. When she meets Dampier, a man unlike anyone she has ever met before, they begin an affair. When he is away with his wife and children at Easter, Anne realises that the unthinkable has happened.

> Fear woke her in the defenceless hour of dawn. She sat up in bed, and faced it at last, shivering so that her teeth chattered, but valiant. She was certain that she was going to have a child.

Anne's stratagems for managing her pregnancy, the baby's birth, and her subsequent life, with or without her lover, are as relevant and heartbreaking today as they would have been a century ago. This novel is remarkable for its period in ignoring moral judgements and for showing Grant's readers the realistic choices that an educated and practical woman has to make when she is thrown on her own resources with an illegitimate baby at the end of the First World War.

Latchkey Ladies (1921) was the first novel by the Canadian author Marjorie Grant Cook. She lived in the UK for most of her adult life, moving back to Canada intermittently for long visits. She was a prolific and influential reviewer for the *Times Literary Supplement*, and published seven novels. She was close friends with Rose Macaulay, whose own secret affair with a married man may have provided the background for Anne Carey's story.

To be published in March 2022.